IRISH
WATERCOLOURS
AND DRAWINGS

THE NATIONAL GALLERY OF IRELAND

DUBLIN 1991

PUBLISHED on the occasion of an exhibition at The National Gallery of Ireland
20 August - 29 September, 1991

British Library Cataloguing in Publication Data
National Gallery of Ireland
Irish Watercolours and Drawings
I. Title
741.9415074

ISBN 0903162563 Pbk
ISBN 0903162571 Hb

EDITED BY Adrian Le Harivel
PHOTOGRAPHY BY John Kellett and Michael Olohan
PRODUCED AND DESIGNED BY Creative Inputs
COLOUR REPRODUCTION AND PRINTING BY Nicholson & Bass

COVER: **Molly Macree** by Thomas Jones (Cat. no. 42)

CONTENTS

Credits	7
Foreword	9
Introduction	10
Catalogue	15
Joseph Samuel Alpenny	16
John James Barralet	18
George Barret	20
Rose Barton	22
Henry Brocas	26
James Henry Brocas	28
Samuel Frederick Brocas	30
Adam Buck	32
James Howard Burgess	34
Frederic William Burton	36
Mildred Anne Butler	40
Patrick Byrne	44
John Henry Campbell	46
Harry Clarke	48
Samuel Dixon	52
Richard Doyle	54
George Victor Du Noyer	56
John Faulkner	58
Thomas Frye	60
Wilhelmina Margaret Geddes	62
George Grattan	64
Nathaniel Grogan	66
Jack P. Hanlon	68
Edward Hayes	70
Michael Angelo Hayes	72
Michael Healy	74

Paul Henry	78
Thomas Hickey	82
Evie Hone	84
Nathaniel Hone The Younger	88
H. Hulley	92
Mainie Jellett	94
Thomas Alfred Jones	98
Harry Kernoff	100
William John Leech	104
Maurice MacGonigal	108
Daniel Maclise	110
James Mahony	112
James Malton	116
William Mulready	120
Henry Newton	122
Andrew Nicholl	124
James George O'Brien	128
William Orpen	130
Walter Frederick Osborne	134
Seán O'Sullivan	138
George Petrie	142
Francis Place	146
Thomas Sautell Roberts	148
Henry Tresham	150
Patrick Tuohy	152
Francis Wheatley	154
Jack Butler Yeats	158
John Butler Yeats	162
Bibliography	166

CREDITS

Catalogue entries are signed with initials and written by:

RK	*Raymond Keaveney*
BPK	*Dr Brian P. Kennedy*
MW	*Dr Michael Wynne*
FC	*Fionnuala Croke*
ALH	*Adrian Le Harivel*

The National Gallery of Ireland has a unique
collection of Irish watercolours and drawings. It
offers a comprehensive survey of the works of
nearly every significant Irish watercolourist and
draughtsman since the seventeenth century. The
collection is not normally on public display for
conservation reasons, but it can be accessed by
making an appointment to visit the Gallery's Print
Room. Some of the watercolours and drawings
are among the most popular images favoured by
our visitors, as confirmed by sales of
reproductions. Consequently, it is a particular
pleasure for the Gallery to host a special
exhibition of our very best Irish watercolours
and drawings.

The range of subject matter included in this
selection offers a potted history of the social and
cultural life of Ireland during the past three
centuries. From a curatorial standpoint, it will be
noticed that the watercolours and drawings are
in superb condition. Any minor matters requiring
attention have been carried out in preparation for
this exhibition by Ms Maighread McParland,
Senior Restorer, and her assistant, Ms Karen
Reihill. The Gallery is grateful to have the
expertise which they bring to the conservation of
watercolours, drawings, prints and miniatures.
All the works were photographed specially for
this exhibition by Mr John Kellett and Mr Michael
Olohan. My colleagues, Dr Brian P. Kennedy,
Assistant Director, Dr Michael Wynne, Keeper,
and Curators, Mr Adrian Le Harivel and Ms
Fionnuala Croke, have joined me in writing this
catalogue. We hope that it will be regarded as an
important scholarly contribution to the study of
Irish watercolours and drawings.

The aim of this exhibition is a popularising one.
We hope that the Irish public and our many
foreign visitors will enjoy these watercolours and
drawings. Some are catalogued here for the first
time, others will be familiar. All, however,
celebrate the fascinating and much under-rated
subject of Irish watercolours and drawings.

Raymond Keaveney
Director

Excepting medieval illuminated manuscripts such as **The Book of Durrow, The Book of Kells, The Corpus Missal** and **The Psalter of Cormac,** the Irish tradition of watercolours and drawings dates only from the 17th century. It emerges from the work of engineers and surveyors such as the military engineer Thomas Phillips (c.1635-1693), sent by Lord Dartmouth to assess ports and their defence systems. He drew maps and nine views in a manuscript of c.1685, now in the National Library of Ireland. Thomas Dineley (c.1664-1695) sketched some towns on a visit in 1680 (also N.L.I.). Francis Place (1647-1728) made a tour of part of Ireland in 1698-99, from Drogheda to Waterford, making a significant number of drawings which record both cities and individual buildings. A fine group is now in the National Gallery of Ireland (N.G.I. 7515-7533). None of these may be considered of high standing as artists; their importance lies in the fact that they preserve images recorded nowhere else.

A major development was the opening of the Dublin Society drawing school in 1746. This subsumed a private school run by Robert West (d.1770). He was supposedly trained in Paris, but only one of his works, an unexceptional oil group portrait at Upton House dated 1735, can be traced today. From the work of his pupils however, it would appear that he taught drawing principally through the medium of chalks, both from the model and classical casts. John James Barralet (c.1747-1815), George Barret (c.1732-1784), Thomas Hickey (1741-1824), Henry Tresham (1750/51-1814), James George O'Brien (fl.1779-1819), George Grattan (1787-1819), Thomas Alfred Jones (1823-1893) - in this catalogue - also Robert Healy (1734-1771), his brother William Healy (fl.1770s), Nathaniel Bermingham (fl.1744-1774), Hugh Douglas Hamilton (1739-1808) and Matthew William Peters (1741-1814) are some of the artists (mainly portraitists) who developed a tremendous facility in the use of chalks, either black and white alone, or coloured.

In landscape painting oils were used predominently. George Barret was an early exponent, but left Ireland for England in 1762. As the rare gouache in this exhibition shows, he was equally competent in this medium. From 1756, the Dublin Society also had a School of Landscape and Ornament run by James Mannin (d.1779). Though intended mainly for craftsmen, John Henry Campbell (1757-1828), John Faulkner (fl.1848-1890), George Petrie (1789-1866), Frederic William Burton (1816-1900) and Francis Danby (1793-1861) all received some training there. Henry Brocas (1766-1838) was the Master from 1800-37. The Society became the Royal Dublin Society in 1820 and its Schools were taken over by the Board of Trade in 1849 becoming later the Metropolitan School of Art, then the National College of Art and Design.

Many Irish artists went to Rome in the eighteenth century, where James Forrester (1730-1776), Hugh Primrose Dean (fl.1758-1784) and Solomon Delane (1727-1812) made some attractive drawings of the city and its environs. Sadly, they are not well represented in the national collections. By contrast, Hugh Douglas Hamilton, whose Roman sojourn was very successful, is shown to advantage in both chalks and oils.

Towards the end of the eighteenth century, Ireland was very well served in the field of landscape watercolour painting by a group of artists, both indigenous and visiting. With a significant interest in individual buildings and street or landscape vistas, one is tempted to compare them in approach, and to a lesser degree in quality, with the great eighteenth century view-painters of Venice and its environs, namely Canaletto, Bellotto, Marieschi and Guardi. Thomas Sautell Roberts (1760-1826) executed twelve watercolours of cities, towns and beauty spots, especially in the south and east of the country. They were engraved in London 1795-99 (N.G.I. 20,838[1-12]) and undoubtedly a larger number would have been completed if the project had met with greater success. Relatively recently a number of the original watercolours have appeared on the market, with their distinctive range of blue colouration. Should one be surprised at the extremely accomplished depiction of Blackrock Castle, or of Blarney Castle, both near Cork? Scarcely, when one considers that the artist was the son of John Roberts, architect of the two cathedrals in Waterford city, and many other fine buildings. Moreover, he studied architecture before dedicating himself to being an artist. Waterford Corporation acquired a beautiful view down the river, showing the old wooden bridge and the waterfront with the merchants' stores and houses. His career as a painter may well have been determined by the premature death, in 1778, of his much older brother Thomas, who painted some of the finest Irish 18th century landscapes in oil.

The watercolours by James Malton (c.1760-1803) in this catalogue are just two from the Gallery's significant holding of such quality studies of major buildings and views in Dublin. Malton came over from England, and arrived when some of Gandon's masterpieces were nearing completion. Malton engraved twenty-five views in aquatint, based on his watercolours. The success of this project was surely due to the fact that the capital of the country was being glorified, and that it was a large centre of population.

Another distinguished English artist, Francis Wheatley (1747-1801), came to Ireland a few years earlier, when he executed some of his finest works in both oil and in watercolour. He fled his creditors in London in 1779, which makes it all the more ironic that it was he who painted the finest interior of the Irish House of Commons, which was dismantled, as part of the agreement, when it was transformed into a banking hall, following the Act of Union of 1801. The painting, executed on a grand scale, now belongs to the City of Leeds Art Gallery.

Wheatley did not reserve his prowess for such elaborate scenes. The famous Donnybrook Fair, then on the outskirts of Dublin, was depicted by him innumerable times, mainly in watercolour. In the catalogue we see a vivid account of the Salmon Leap at Leixlip, County Kildare (Cat. no. 71). Showing a more formal subject is the watercolour of Speaker Pery entering the House of Commons, in solemn fashion (Cat. no. 70). The great portico is a superb setting, but a number of citizens represented are certainly not being reverential to this event. Wheatley returned to London in 1783, fleeing a different group of creditors. Landscapists such as John Henry Campbell (1757-1828) and H. Hulley (fl. 1783-1790) are more shadowy artists.

From the late eighteenth century a great interest developed in recording antiquities, the study of which was to continue and develop, flourishing right down to the present day. Prehistory and the early Christian period were the focus of attention. Anything after the late seventeenth century was ignored by the scholars. Eighteenth century houses on a grand scale were where some people lived, and it was too soon to study the great public buildings in the cities. Fortunately, as has been seen, some of the artists did not ignore them. Much of the art related to the antiquarian movement was pragmatic and minor, but nonetheless vitally important. A number of artists turned their antiquarian records into a genuine art form. Notable among these was George Petrie (1789-1866) and one of his pupils, George Victor Du Noyer (1817-1869), both represented in the catalogue. The nineteenth century saw a great flowering of the art of watercolour painting in both Great Britain and Ireland. In topographical work, Irish artists like Andrew Nicholl (1804-1886), James Howard Burgess (c.1817-1890), Henry Newton (fl.1840-1856) and John Faulkner (fl.1848-1890) often included an important building or ancient monument, or depicted a place with historic associations.

For a rather unusual approach to subjects, a special place must be kept for James Mahony (1810-1879). His panoramic view of Dublin (Cat. no. 49), taken from the spire of St George's Church, north of the Liffey, is a formidable piece of draughtsmanship, giving us a remarkably detailed panorama of Dublin in 1854. There are many other fascinating works by him, including expansive views inside Dublin's Irish Industrial Exhibition of 1853 (N.G.I. 2452, 2453 and Cat. no. 50).

The High Victorian era also saw a blossoming of watercolours describing events from legend or later literature. Among the Irish exponents of this genre, Frederic William Burton was a consummate practitioner. Daniel Maclise, apart from his individual compositions, was employed to illustrate books. William Mulready (1786-1863), whose family emigrated from County Clare, was also a master with both pencil and watercolour. He is quite rightly renowned for his figure studies; throughout his career he returned to draw from the live figure at regular intervals, in order to maintain a high standard in all his figurative works.

As well as the truly professional artists, there was a galaxy of amateurs, principally ladies, some of whom were more accomplished than their avowedly professional contemporaries. One example is sufficient: the work of Louisa, Marchioness of Waterford (1818-1891) , is collected for its artistic merit, rather than for her aristocratic title. Moving towards the later nineteenth century, Ireland produced two professional female watercolourists, Rose Barton (1856-1929) and Mildred Anne Butler (1858-1941). The former was never really forgotten, largely on account of the reproduction of a considerable number of her views. Mildred Anne Butler is rather a latter day rediscovery, because of the sale of a large number of her works, following the death of a cousin who owned Kilmurry, County Kilkenny, where the artist had lived and had her studio.

The excellent pencil sketches of John Butler Yeats (1839-1922), taken during meetings or dinners, have left us with likenesses of a vast array of interesting people. On occasion he also painted a theme from poetry (Cat. no. 75). His son Jack B. Yeats (1871-1957), arguably Ireland's greatest artist, is remembered mainly for his fine expressionist-style oil paintings. He started his career working almost exclusively in watercolours. Of particular interest today are the records he made of life in the West of Ireland (Cat. no. 72). Like Yeats there are many artists who bridge the nineteenth and twentieth centuries. Walter Osborne (1859-1903) is one of these and although he died suddenly aged forty-three he has given us some remarkable watercolours. Those in which children appear are quite enchanting, and deservedly extremely popular.

William Orpen (1878-1931) was a master of the line; his pencil figure studies, as of fellow artist Oliver Sheppard (Cat. no. 59), clearly demonstrate this proficiency. He was also a compulsive caricaturist, embellishing many of his letters with visual anecdotal sketches or self-portraits. Many of his large compositions, or portions of them, were developed in line and watercolour (Cat. no. 58). The influence of years spent studying and working on the Continent is apparent in the development of a number of Irish artists represented in the catalogue. Nathaniel Hone (1831-1917) spent many years with leading figures of the Barbizon school. Paul Henry's (1876-1958) dignified portraits of Mayo men and women undoubtedly owe a debt to Millet's sympathetic description of French peasant life. Through Mainie Jellett (1897-1944), a most excellent teacher, the influence of cubism reached Ireland. One of her most notable pupils was Jack Hanlon (1913-1968), who was most expressive in watercolour.

Ireland has been well served by its artists in portraiture in the first half of the twentieth century. Very fine indeed, and good likenesses, are the pencil or chalk drawings by Seán

O'Sullivan (1906-1964). He recorded a wide range of sitters, both in political and artistic circles. One cannot leave an account of this period without referring to the important stained glass movement. On one side there is Harry Clarke (1889-1931), who, like other artists in this medium, had to provide sketch designs of projected windows. Aside from his stained glass work, Harry Clarke could be remembered alone for his monochrome and colour illustrations in a number of publications, especially a series of nine for the publisher Harrap's. Clarke has been called the Irish Aubrey Beardsley, but this is far too simplistic an analysis. There are similarities, but Clarke drew on a wider range of source material, not least his native Ireland. The work of his cousin Maurice MacGonigal (1900-1979) evolved in a very different fashion (Cat. no. 47).

Michael Healy (1873-1941) was a founder member of **An Túr Gloine** co-operative stained glass works. Already a fully trained artist, he was initiated into the difficult glass medium by Alfred Ernest Child (1875-1939) who had come over to manage the studio, and to teach at the Dublin Metropolitan School of Art. Much of Healy's output was sent abroad to England, Canada, the USA (Cat. no. 30) and New Zealand. Healy never abandoned his habit of sketching, with ever so light colour washes, the people of Dublin, and the countryside around. One could not reconstruct the city and its people from these; what they do convey is mood and atmosphere.

Michael Healy was the person in **An Túr Gloine** who gave Evie Hone (1894-1955) the warmest welcome, and assistance in matters of technique. Evie Hone's sketch designs are broader in treatment, using her preferred medium of gouache, with the lead lines frequently indicated by chinese ink. She made many studies of gardens, views of agreeable scenery, and recorded, usually in ink alone, scenes from High Crosses, or later medieval carvings. The stained glass artists of **An Túr**

Gloine gained an international reputation for Ireland in this field.

Whether as a preliminary study or finished piece, Irish artists have created watercolours and drawings of a range and quality which warrant serious attention. This catalogue, and other recent publications, will, it is hoped, assist the enjoyment and study of this hitherto undervalued side of Irish art.

CATALOGUE

JOSEPH SAMUEL ALPENNY

Southern Ireland 1787 - 1858 London

Of obscure origin in the south of Ireland, Alpenny was in London by 1804 when he received a premium from the Society of Arts for a drawing, followed by a silver palette for another in 1808. He then called himself Halfpenny and exhibited at the Royal Academy 1805-08. In 1810, he sent three works from Waterford to The Society of Artists of the City of Dublin exhibition. By 1812 he had moved to 13, St Andrew's Street, Dublin and changed his name to Alpenny. His most productive years were from 1812-21 when he exhibited a myriad of subjects. Apart from landscape views of Counties Wicklow, Waterford, Tipperary and Kilkenny, there were mythological and religious themes and illustrations to Walter Scott's poem **Lady of the Lake.** From 1821-23 he lived at 99, Great Britain Street and exhibited also in Limerick and Cork. In 1823 he exhibited, and published his own etching of, **The Entrance of George IV into Dublin on 17th August, 1821.** He is next found in London at Kew, moving later to Richmond and Clapham, and exhibiting occasionally at the Royal Academy until 1853. In 1825 Ackermann published Alpenny's **New Drawing Book of Rustic Figures** with four lithographs by him.

1 Portrait of Edward Hayes, 1812

WATERCOLOUR OVER PENCIL ON PAPER 41 x 29.2 cms.

SIGNED AND DATED lower left, J.S. Alpenny. 1812

PROVENANCE Purchased from Mr J.G. Robertson, 1883. N.G.I. 2002.

EXHIBITED ?Dublin 1813 (202); Dallas 1976 (27).

LITERATURE Strickland 1913, vol. 1, pp. 6 and 458 (illus. opp. p. 460); Thieme-Becker 1923, vol. xvi, p. 174; Mallalieu 1979, vol. 2, p. 298 (illus.); Le Harivel 1983, p. 2 (illus.).

This is a portrait of the artist Edward Hayes (1797-1864), painted when he was only fifteen and studying drawing with Alpenny. It may well be *A youth sketching from nature* exhibited at the fourth and final exhibition of the Society of Artists of the City of Dublin in 1813. Hayes came from County Tipperary and studied at the Dublin Society Schools. It is not known precisely how long he studied with Alpenny. Hayes exhibited at the R.H.A. from 1830, while living in Waterford and teaching, and having moved to Dublin the next year, built a successful career painting miniatures and landscapes (Cat. no. 28). Alpenny's rather limited technique gives a naive charm to this amusing, if unlikely, image of a well-dressed young man who is seated on the riverbank to earnestly sketch the prospect. His top hat serves to rest a sheet of paper on. The impression is more of a studio photograph with a landscape backdrop. The locale appears to be the densely forested, hilly terrain of County Wicklow near the river Dargle and Powerscourt House demesne, which was frequented by artists and tourists from the mid-18th century onwards. Only a day's excursion from Dublin, it offered material ranging from the picturesque to the sublime. The distant mountain recalls the Great Sugar Loaf, the highest peak in County Wicklow. Alpenny works with thin, flat washes of colour, which are somewhat faded. The main underdrawing is on his sitter's face and hands. His depiction of trees owes much to George Barret and Jonathan Fisher.

ALH

JOHN JAMES BARRALET

Dublin *c. 1747 - 1815* Philadelphia

John James Barralet studied with James Mannin, the landscape master at the Dublin Society Schools and, having worked in Dublin for some years, in 1770 he went to London where he was reasonably successful, partly earning his living by teaching. Apparently not happy with the measure of success in London, he returned to Ireland in 1779. He worked in Dublin until 1795, when he left for America, settling in Philadelphia where he was employed as a book illustrator. He remained in Philadelphia for the rest of his life. Very few of Barralet's original works are known to survive, but his quality and style can be judged from engravings after his works.

2 The banks of the river Liffey, near Lucan, County Dublin, 1782

WATERCOLOUR ON PAPER 25.5 x 40.7 cms.

SIGNED AND DATED lower left, *J J Barralet 1782*

INSCRIBED on backing paper, lower right, *No 59. R Dublin Society Ed Hardman/Asist Secr. 1833.*

PROVENANCE Royal Dublin Society, probably purchased on 12 December 1833 (Turpin 1986, p. 49); acquired by the State 1877 and lodged in the National Museum of Ireland until transferred in 1966. N.G.I. 3884.

LITERATURE McGoogan 1915, p. 13, no. 17 (illus. opp. p. 5); Le Harivel 1983, p. 6 (illus.).

This view is taken on the left bank of the river Liffey between Lucan and Chapelizod, on a stretch known as the Strawberry Beds. Because, in the centre of the watercolour, in the middle ground, a demesne wall leading to a small gate can be seen, it has been suggested that this is the not dissimilar entry to Luttrellstown Castle. The main gate of the Castle at this point is recessed from the road, and is situated at a break in a densely wooded area.

An old castle of the Pale, the property of the Luttrell family, which produced both notorious and distinguished members, Luttrellstown Castle remained in the family until about 1800 when General Henry Luttrell, 2nd Earl of Carhampton, sold it to Luke White, MP, who transformed it into a much grander residence. Luke White's son was created Lord Annaly, and this family retained ownership for over a century. Its most recent owner was the Hon. Mrs Aileen Plunket, who received it as a marriage gift from her father, the Hon. Ernest Guinness. A few years ago Mrs Plunket sold the castle, and one of the most beautiful demesnes in Ireland, with fine land, beautiful timber and a large lake. This watercolour, numbered 59 on the backing paper, may be among sixty landscape and figurative subjects purchased by the Royal Dublin Society Schools in 1833 at a cost of £40. Watteau landscapes (N.G.I. 3822-3823) were 51 and 48; a Ricci (N.G.I. 3979) was 60.

MW

GEORGE BARRET, R.A.

Dublin c.1732 · 1784 London

George Barret attended Robert West's drawing school in Dublin. Edmund Burke saw his work, and urged him to study from nature; from this period came some of his superb landscape paintings in oils in and around the Powerscourt demesne, County Wicklow. Disappointed with patronage in Dublin, Barret went to London and exhibited there from 1763. He was very successful, receiving major commissions from, amongst others, the Reverend John Lock of Norbury Park, the Duke of Portland at Welbeck and the Duke of Argyll at Inveraray. Despite earning about two thousand pounds a year, he managed to spend more. A foundation member of the Royal Academy, in 1768, his style appealed to such an extent that the superbly accomplished Richard Wilson had great trouble in earning even a modest living. On his death Barret left no provision for his wife, but the Royal Academy filled the need by giving his widow a pension.

3 Ullswater, Cumberland, c.1780

GOUACHE ON PAPER LAID DOWN ON LINEN 51 x 66 cms.

SIGNED on *verso, George Barret*

ENGRAVED by Samuel Middiman, 1784, for **Select Views in Great Britain** (1784-92), plate 6.

PROVENANCE Professor J.V. Rice, Leixlip, County Kildare, from whom purchased 1975. N.G.I. 7736.

EXHIBITED Dallas 1976 (5).

LITERATURE Bodkin 1920, p. 3; Crookshank and Glin 1978, p. 119, plate 24; Le Harivel 1983, p. 6 (illus.). Gillespie, Mooney and Ryan 1986, p. 4 (illus.); Butler p. 55, fig. 49.

One of very few works by Barret known to have been executed in this medium, the view of one of the beauty spots in the Lake District is handled with great skill and confidence. Middiman describes the view as of Hollin Fell (centre) on its bold promontory, taken from fern topped Soulby Fell, with 'the vast chaos of mountains that guard the Head of the lake' beyond. It is possible that the gouache itself was not used for the engraving mentioned above. More brittle than egg shell, the gouache, painted on paper stretched on thin linen, becomes an extremely fragile work of art. Before, or indeed after the gouache, Barret could have given the engraver a pencil drawing. His pencil drawings from nature are extremely fine and quite numerous. Watercolours, on the contrary, are not plentiful. A similar lake scene (also with a boat transporting cattle) is dated 22 February 1781 (Mallalieu 1990, illus. p. 100).

Apart from **Ullswater, Cumberland,** Samuel Middiman included two other plates after Barret in his **Select Views in Great Britain,** namely **Winnandermere** [sic] **Lake, Westmoreland** and **View on Shanklin Cline.** Barret did the originals for six plates of **Seats of the Nobility and Gentry** (1779-86), published by another artist, William Watts. In the present context, it is of interest to note that Barret himself etched at least three plates: **View in the Dargle, View of Hawarden** (1773), and **Landscape with figures.**

MW

ROSE BARTON, R.W.S.

Dublin 1856 - 1929 London

Rose Barton was, like her life-long friend
*Mildred Anne Butler, one of a number of late
nineteenth century young ladies who pursued
the socially acceptable activity of painting, but
should be regarded as professional artists who
took their work seriously, studying abroad and
exhibiting regularly. Barton's father was a
lawyer from Rochestown, County Tipperary. She
and her elder sister, Emily Alma, were
educated at home by a German governess who
also instructed them in drawing and music. In
1874 their father died and Rose travelled with
her mother and sister to Brussels where Rose
took lessons in painting and drawing. In France
she studied with Henri Gervex where she
learnt the techniques of Impressionist painting
and acquired many of the characteristics which
remained with her throughout her career, her
preference for bright colours and plein-air
painting and 'a certain impressionistic
woolliness of outline' (Cork, London, Belfast
and Kilkenny 1987, introduction). Back in
Dublin, Rose exhibited for the first time in 1878
at the Royal Hibernian Academy, and from
1880 she was exhibiting in a number of London
galleries, including the Dudley Gallery, the
Society of Lady Artists and the Royal Academy.
She was made an Associate of the Royal
Watercolour Society in 1893, but was not
elected a full member here until 1911. Also an
illustrator, Rose contributed to Frances Gerard's
(the pseudonym of Geraldine Fitzgerald)* **Dublin
Old and New,** *and in 1904 she provided sixty-
one illustrations and an accompanying text for*
Familiar London. *From 1904 she lived in
Knightsbridge until her death in 1929. She
enjoyed visits from her young relations who
remember with affection her absent
mindedness, and fondness for betting and
horse-racing.*

4 Going to the Levée, 1897

WATERCOLOUR ON PAPER 35.6 x 26.6 cms.

SIGNED AND DATED lower right, *Rose Barton 1897*

PROVENANCE Said to have been bought at the Royal Hibernian Academy, though
not exhibited; presented by Miss R. Harricks, 1947. N.G.I. 2989.

EXHIBITED Dublin 1970 (99); Dallas 1976 (59); Cork, London, Belfast and Kilkenny
1987 (17); Dublin 1987 (45); Dublin 1988 (-).

LITERATURE Le Harivel 1983, p. 9 (illus.); Gillespie, Mooney and Ryan 1986, p. 40
(illus.); Butler 1990, p. 155.

In 1892, Rose Barton and her sister Emily Alma were presented at Dublin
Castle, an event she recorded five years later in this watercolour. The Levée
was an afternoon party only given by the Lord Lieutenant during the Winter
Season at the Castle, an event of considerable importance in Dublin Society. She
illustrates the moment of arrival at the Castle. A sweep of carriages turns from
Dame Street into Cork Hill and through the gate below Van Nost the Younger's
statue of Justice. Their arrival is watched with great interest by the crowd of
men, women and children who stand on either side of the road. The scene is
shrouded in a winter mist, characteristic of the artist's views of London, and
indicative of the influence of Whistler in her work. The overall blue, grey and
brown tonality is relieved by the use of yellow highlights and two women's
bright red jackets. Blobs of flesh colour paint form the anonymous faces of the
crowd. The rooftops follow the outline of the buildings in Cork Hill and the
Castle in the background with the salt-cellar shape of Bedford Tower looming
up on the right. There is a smaller version of the watercolour dated 1906
(private collection) and a similar view (taken from a grey wash drawing) was
reproduced in **Dublin Old and New** (1898, p. 21).

FC

ROSE BARTON, R.W.S.

Dublin 1856 - 1929 *London*

5 Hop Pickers in Kent returning home, 1894

WATERCOLOUR ON PAPER 34.7 x 26.7 cms.

SIGNED AND DATED lower left, *Rose Barton. 1894*

PROVENANCE By descent to the artist's nephew, Raymond F. Brooke, and bequeathed by him, 1952. N.G.I. 3259.

EXHIBITED R.W.S. Winter Exhibition 1894-95 (154); Cork, London, Belfast and Kilkenny 1987 (17); Dublin 1987 (46).

Although titled *Hop Pickers in Kent returning home* the landscape is undefined, consisting of a haze of green field meeting a pink evening sky. The centre of the picture is rendered with broad washes of blue and pink blurring to a pale purple. These hues are relieved by occasional smudges of flesh tones and the russet brown in one of the women's aprons.

Two women and a young girl are walking home across this field. At second glance we realise that the first woman is weighed down by a child wrapped in a blanket on her back, identified by the pink bonnet and its legs and boots hanging down. These 'impressionistic' figures are painted with the same washes as the landscape, their skirts merging with the brushstrokes of the grassy field.

This smudging of forms, or use of a haze, is evident also in Rose Barton's urban scenes. The avoidance of detail heightens the mood of the scene - the silence and calm at the end of the day - and by concentrating on the forms she evokes the sense of toil and weariness in the three figures.

FC

Rose Barton.
1894.

HENRY BROCAS

Dublin 1766 - 1837 *Dublin*

Brocas was a self-taught artist who mainly painted landscape watercolours. He was also a busy engraver of portraits, political caricatures and other subjects for Dublin magazines from the 1780s. He made prints after Gainsborough and Reynolds and illustrated an edition of the Bible (1793). He exhibited in Dublin from 1800-12, and at the R.H.A. in 1830. Brocas was appointed Master of the School of Landscape and Ornament at the Dublin Society Schools in 1800, but was criticised for being remiss in his duties, from 1811 onwards. Following public reproofs in 1830-31, his salary was reduced and he stopped teaching, due to ill-health, in 1837. His son, Henry Brocas Junior, offered to take over his duties, and mustered sufficient votes to defeat Andrew Nicholl (in spite of the Fine Arts Committee recommending him), when the new Master was voted on by the Society. Three other sons of Henry Brocas, James Henry, Samuel Frederick and William, were also artists.

6 Carlingford Castle, County Louth

WATERCOLOUR ON PAPER 29.5 x 42 cms.

INSCRIBED lower left, *714-84* (National Museum of Ireland inventory number) on partial stamp, *Dublin*

PROVENANCE Royal Dublin Society, probably from the artist; acquired by the State 1877 and lodged in the National Museum of Ireland until transferred in 1966. N.G.I. 3889.

LITERATURE McGoogan 1915, p. 15, no. 23; Le Harivel 1983, p. 23 (illus.); de Courcy and Maher 1985, p. 33 (illus.).

Located sixty miles north of Dublin, Carlingford Castle was built in the 12th century by the Norman, Hugh de Lacy, to dominate the entrance to Carlingford Lough. It is popularly known as King John's Castle, following his three day visit in 1210. A spur of rock above a natural harbour decided the unusual design. The near side is semicircular, with a rectangular tower at the south-west corner and the remains of gate towers, which flanked a narrow entrance. The straight eastern half was added in 1261. Much damage was caused by 17th century sieges. The village grew up by the castle and includes a Mint (1467), Tholsel, and Taaffe's Castle, the 16th century fortified house seen here. Majestic Slieve Foye rises in the distance, with the Mourne Mountains across the Bay. In 1837 there were 288 houses in the town. As part of his duties as Master of the School of Landscape and Ornament at the Dublin Society schools, Brocas had to regularly supply drawings for copying and this may have been produced for that purpose. He exhibited views of castles in Counties Donegal and Down at the Society of Artists of Ireland in 1804 and may have visited Carlingford on the same trip. It is typical of his work in the application of broad strokes of colour, with little specific detail even in the foreground, and distant shapes such as the castle, merging into the blues of the mountain and sky. Fishing boats are a particular Brocas motif, here appropriate given Carlingford's renown for herrings. Figures appear to be gathering the local oysters. It is difficult to date watercolours by Brocas as they are hardly ever dated and his style remains consistent, principally a reaction against the technique of 18th century topographical watercolours which continued to influence the work of his sons.

ALH

JAMES HENRY BROCAS

Dublin c.1790 - 1846 *Cork*

The eldest son of Henry Brocas, he studied in the Dublin Society Schools, winning prizes in 1802-03, plus a medal for etching. He contributed etchings of cattle to the Dublin Society's **Survey of Co. Dublin** *(1802) and exhibited landscapes and portraits of prize cattle and horses, in Dublin, from 1801-10. He had presumably visited Wales by 1814 when he exhibited two views from around Mount Snowdon. Little else is known except that he moved to Cork about 1834. Portraits by him were exhibited posthumously at the 1852 Cork Exhibition.*

7 Old Baal's Bridge, Limerick, c.1810

WATERCOLOUR OVER INK ON PAPER 23.3 x 39.5 cms.

PROVENANCE Purchased from Mr Lionel Marks, London, 1904. N.G.I. 2559.

EXHIBITED Dublin 1975 (113); Dallas 1976 (28)

LITERATURE Rothery 1978, p. 18 (illus.); Le Harivel 1983, p. 24 (illus.); de Courcy and Maher 1985, p. 44 (illus.); Butler 1990, fig. 37; O'Keefe and Simington 1991, pp. 149, 151.

This is a fascinating record of a part of Limerick, now completely destroyed. Old Baal's Bridge, which actually had four arches, was a medieval bridge linking the separate communities of Irishtown and Englishtown (the latter around the castle and cathedral) across the Abbey river. Beyond can be seen shipping by the Custom House on the river Shannon. Unusually the bridge was privately owned and from the 17th century there were two rows of houses and shops, separated only by a narrow walkway. In 1761, Viscount Shannon sold the east side to the government who demolished them to reveal one half of the street. There was flood damage in 1775, but the glazed shopfronts, attached to Georgian brick facades, indicate that prosperity returned. The substantial mansion on the left in Irishtown shows the impact of the late 18th century extension to the city, Newtown Pery, while beyond there are two gabled late 17th century 'Dutch billy' houses, a type once widespread in Dublin. Brocas has caught the atmosphere of a busy provincial town about 1810, as the postchaise (with King George III's monogram) arrives, a carter delivers turf, and barrels in the street wait to be moved. The bridge was demolished and rebuilt as Ball's Bridge in 1831. Brocas records detail with the swift strokes of an etcher, before applying colour like Malton or Wheatley in the 18th century. He clearly disliked drawing figures, almost repeating the woman with her load four times. His perspective is a little weak, but there is an interest in quirky detail that makes this unique townscape by him very memorable. W.H. Bartlett's c.1830 view of the bridge was lithographed for *The Scenery and Antiquities of Ireland* (1842).

ALH

SAMUEL FREDERICK BROCAS

Dublin c.1792 - 1847 Dublin

The second son of Henry Brocas, he attended the Dublin Society Schools winning medals for flower painting in 1801, etching 1801 and figure drawing 1807. He exhibited pictures of prize cattle, portraits and a Welsh view, in Dublin 1809-12 and landscapes at the R.H.A. 1832-47, predominately of the Powerscourt Estate, County Wicklow and its environs and of Killarney. Most of his work was in watercolour. Twelve of his views of Dublin were engraved by his brother Henry Brocas the Younger (1798-1873), and issued 1818-28. This was both to rival Malton's views of the city and as part of a projected series **The Topography of Ireland,** *which never came about. He published his own lithograph of* **King John's Castle, Limerick,** *in 1826.*

8 Trinity College and College Green, Dublin, 1818

INK AND WATERCOLOUR ON PAPER 24.4 x 40.2 cms.

SIGNED AND DATED lower right, *S. BROCAS delt Dublin 1818*

ETCHED by Henry Brocas the Younger, published J. Le Petit, Dublin 1829 (N.G.I. 11,956, hand-coloured).

PROVENANCE Purchased from Mr Lionel Marks, London, 1904. N.G.I. 2558.

LITERATURE Strickland 1913, vol. 1, p. 94; Le Harivel 1983, p. 25 (illus.); de Courcy and Maher 1985, p. 14 (illus.); Butler 1990, p. 41, fig. 39.

Trinity College was founded in 1592 by Queen Elizabeth I, but only received its present facade 1752-59, to a design by gentleman architect Theodore Jacobsen. His only other major building was the (now demolished) Foundling Hospital in London. He intended there to be a dome above the Regent's House in the centre, which leads into Front Square where the Chapel and Examination Hall were later added. Wicklow granite is set off by Portland stone dressings; the ornament carved by David Sheehan. The Irish Parliament was swayed to allay the high costs, and with the opening up of College Green to the river and also towards Merrion Square, by the Wide Street Commissioners, a suitably grand central area of the city was created. In the distance can be seen the stone gates of the Provost's House, which is mostly hidden. Malton had earlier depicted the same view, and while Brocas is a lesser draughtsman, working on a smaller scale, like his brother James Henry Brocas he records architectural detail and figures with swift penstrokes over which he applies light washes of colour. Responsive to the fall of light on a building he has an equally alert eye for capturing the street life. The man accompanying a well-dressed lady in an enormous hat; lecturers from Trinity College; a woman with her parasol; men riding and the man carrying a load, all contribute to the sense of place. In the etching Henry Brocas the Younger reproduces the scene almost exactly (even to the colouring), but the figures have become stylized and the architecture somewhat askew. To give a more Irish feel, he replaced the monogram on the nearer coach by a harp and suppressed the 'Bank of England' sign on a corner house. A third brother, William Brocas (c.1794-1868), had a *View of Trinity College and East Portico of the Bank of Ireland* lithographed by Havell and Son (N.G.I. 11,646).

ALH

ADAM BUCK

Cork 1759 - 1833 London

Son of a Cork silversmith, Jonathan Buck, his early career is undocumented, but he was probably self-taught and became an accomplished miniature painter in Cork. He may have come to Dublin but had gone permanently to London by 1795 when he exhibited marine views (now lost) at the Royal Academy. He continued to exhibit, until 1833, once as many as one hundred and seventy-two works. Buck also exhibited twice at the British Institution and three times at the Society of British Artists. His sitters were generally politicians, clergy, military officers and actors. Apart from miniatures he also showed small full-length portraits in watercolour and subjects to be engraved. Buck planned to publish his own etchings of Greek vases but only issued ten prints in 1812; he also provided drawings which were aquatinted in colour for an edition of Sterne's *Sentimental Journey*. His son Sidney Buck tried to follow his father but is now forgotten, while his brother Frederick Buck (1771-1840) had a successful career as a less sophisticated miniature painter in Cork.

9 Portrait of a Lady with an artist's folio, 1803

WATERCOLOUR OVER BLACK CHALK ON PAPER 39 x 29 cms.

SIGNED AND DATED lower right, *Adam Buck 1803 London*

PROVENANCE Douglas Wing, Rye (1961); presented by Mr Maurice Fridberg, 1975. N.G.I. 7738.

EXHIBITED Dallas 1976 (12).

LITERATURE Le Harivel 1983, p. 27 (illus.); Dublin 1984, no. 17; Gillespie, Mooney and Ryan 1986, p. 16 (illus.).

An unidentified lady in startling blue dress, stands on a terrace with a half open artist's folio open on a chair. She has been called 'Countess Danvers' in the past, but there is nothing to substantiate this. Buck used a similar composition and background for the **Countess of Cavan** (1805, location unknown) and clearly found that small whole-length portraits such as these were very popular in London. Some are in pure watercolour, others are over chalk, while a third type, according to his contemporary Anthony Pasquin, was drawn in a wax crayon that he invented. Here, there is light underdrawing on the dress, folio and carpet in black chalk, with white highlights on the dress in gouache. The facial modelling is done as if he was still miniature painting on ivory, while the background wrought iron balustrade and carpet are less defined. In keeping with Buck's liking for Antique art, the Empire dress, shoes, hairstyle, chair in the style of Thomas Hope, and ornamental work, are all in the neo-classical style of the period.

ALH

JAMES HOWARD BURGESS

? Belfast c.1817 - 1890 *Belfast*

*Little biographical information is available about this painter of mainly topographical subjects. He exhibited at the Royal Hibernian Academy from 1830 and was a drawing master in Belfast by 1841, when twenty-five of his views were engraved for Hall's **Ireland, its scenery, character etc.** (1841-43). Strickland knew of miniatures by him and he is listed in the 1843-44 Belfast **Post Office Directory** as a landscape and animal painter. He illustrated an edition of Moore's **Melodies** (1845), and Ward's **Progressive book of landscape drawing** (1848) and **Views in the North of Ireland** (1862). He lithographed a seascape by Kendrick, at Carrickfergus, in 1846. During the 1850s he ran a drawing Academy in Donegall Place, Belfast and was closely involved with the Harbour Commissioners, making lithographs of harbour developments. Burgess also painted in Yorkshire, Wales and Scotland.*

10 Dunluce Castle, County Antrim

WATERCOLOUR ON PAPER 53 x 78.8 cms.

SIGNED AND DATED lower left, *J. Howard Burgess. 1866*

PROVENANCE Presented by the Reverend J.R. McKee, Oxford, 1922. N.G.I. no. 7332.

LITERATURE Le Harivel 1983, p. 29 (illus.); de Courcy and Maher 1985, p. 35 (illus.).

About two and half miles west of the town of Bushmills is ruined Dunluce Castle, a formidable structure built c.1300 by Richard de Burge, Earl of Ulster. The castle occupies the top of a detached basaltic rock and is separated from the mainland by a deep twenty foot-wide chasm. Its stormy history in the hands of the de Mandevilles, who are better known by their Irish name of McQuillan, came to an end when it was taken and reconstructed by the Scottish McDonnells c.1560. The Earl of Antrim, who lives in Glenarm Castle and is the representative McDonnell today, handed the ruins over to the State.

The castle is a good example of Anglo-Norman architecture and features five circular towers joined by a strong curtain wall. A platform on the inside of the wall allowed archers to fire through openings in the battlements. Remains include two of the original towers and fragments of two others, plus a large rectangular gatehouse at the south-west angle as well as extensive domestic buildings. The gatehouse dates from c.1600 and takes the place of the keep which the castle never had - probably because of its cliff-top position. Round turrets of the Scottish type still crown the outer angles of this later structure.

MW

FREDERIC WILLIAM BURTON, R.H.A.

Corofin 1816 - 1900 London

Frederic William Burton was the son of amateur landscape artist Samuel Frederick Burton of Corofin House, County Clare, a fact which would most likely have facilitated his own aspirations to become a painter. Another factor which may have influenced his choice of career was an accident he had in childhood which severely injured his right arm. Following his family's removal to Dublin in 1826, Frederic (his preferred spelling) enrolled in the Dublin Society Schools, where he studied under Henry Brocas and Robert Lucius West. In 1832, his watercolour Abraham on his journey to sacrifice Isaac was exhibited at the RHA and he continued to exhibit there regularly until 1861. His artistic education was complemented by contact with many of the most notable Irish intellectuals of the day, including George Petrie, Sir Samuel Ferguson, Professor Eugene O'Curry and Dr William Stokes. He developed an interest in the Irish countryside and its landscape, the customs and dress of the people and its archaeology. Over the period 1838-41 he accompanied Petrie on his ethnological expedition to the Aran Islands. In 1851 he left for Germany, and spent seven years in the employ of Maximilian II of Bavaria, during which time he gained extensive knowledge of Old Master painting. On his return from the Continent in 1858, he settled in London, where, in 1874, he was appointed Director of the National Gallery, a post he held until 1894. He died in London, March 1900, and was buried in the family plot at Mount Jerome cemetery in Dublin.

11 The Meeting on the Turret Stairs, 1864

WATERCOLOUR ON PAPER 95.5 x 60.8 cms.

SIGNED AND DATED lower left, FWB 1864

PROVENANCE Sold by the artist to dealer Edward Fox White, 1864; purchased by J.W. Knight, 1864; bought from Knight by Agnew's, 1866; John Knowles (Manchester watercolours collector) sale, Christie's, 7 May 1877, lot 67, bought by J. Grant Morris (through Vokins); J. Grant Morris sale, Christie's, 23-25 April 1898, lot 7, bought by Agnew's; sold to Miss Margaret Stokes, 1898, by whom bequeathed, 1900. NGI 2358.

EXHIBITED O.W.S. 1864 (82); Dublin 1865 (56); Dublin 1900 (19); London 1913 (82); Cork 1971 (16); Columbus, Toledo and St Louis 1974 (9); Dallas 1976 (44).

LITERATURE D.N.B. 1901, p. 347; Haight 1955; MacFarlane 1976, p. 15; Crookshank and Glin 1978, p. 243, plate 50,; Harbison, Potterton and Sheehy 1978, p. 214, plate 35; Crookshank 1979 p. 52 (illus.); Le Harivel 1983, p. 31 (illus.); Gillespie, Mooney and Ryan 1986, p. 29 (illus.); Bourke 1987 pp. 33-34 (illus.); Christie's sale 27 October 1987, lot 162; Bourke 1988, p. 193 (illus.); Dublin 1988a, pp. 116-17, fig. 55a; Butler 1990, p. 147. N.G.I. 1990, p. 116, fig. 2.

'My father gave me a glorious guard;
Twelve noble knights were my watch and ward.
Eleven daily served me well,
But oh, I loved the last - I fell...

They stood at the door with spear and shield:
"Up Lord HILDEBRAND! out and yield!"
He kissed me then mine eyes above:-
"Say never my name, thou darling love"
Out of the door Lord Hildebrand sprang;
around his head the sword he swang...'

The illustration of an episode from a Danish ballad, translated by Whitley Stokes and published in *Fraser's Magazine* of January 1855, is somewhat exceptional for an artist who rarely treated literary subjects. This masterpiece represents, in brilliant colour, reminiscent of the Pre-Raphaelite School, the ill-fated relationship between Hellelil and the Prince of Engellend, Hildebrand, one of her bodyguards, who part here for the last time. Their tragic love results in the slaying of seven of Hellelil's brothers by Hildebrand and his own death at the hand of the youngest. George Eliot praised Burton, writing 'Only through a great deal of suffering could anyone have worked his way to such height as you have gained in this picture'. It was obviously a very ambitious undertaking as is evidenced by many preparatory studies. Twenty-four were included in Burton's posthumous sale at Christie's (21 June 1901); a colour study, Hellelil in a green dress, came to light more recently. There are a full-scale drawing (N.G.I. 2384), oversize wash study (N.G.I. 2386), small pencil sketch (N.G.I. 19,352) and drapery study (N.G.I. 6825) already in the collection.

RK

12 Portrait of Miss Annie Callwell, 1840s

WATERCOLOUR ON PAPER 59.1 x 40.6 cms.

PROVENANCE Bequeathed by the sitter, 1904. N.G.I. 6030.

EXHIBITED Dublin 1900 (56); Dublin, London and Belfast 1969-70 (115); Dallas 1976 (46).

LITERATURE Crookshank and Glin 1978, p. 244, fig. 241; Le Harivel 1983, p. 36 (illus.); Butler 1990, p. 148.

During the period when he submitted paintings to the R.H.A., Burton exhibited over fifty portraits. The present work represents Miss Annie Callwell (d.1904), daughter of Robert Callwell, who served on the first Board of the National Gallery of Ireland until his death in 1871. Burton depicts her out of doors, seated against a wooded landscape surrounded by flowers and reeds. The pose, look and surroundings, vaguely recall Pierre-Paul Prud'hon's portrait of the Empress Josephine (1805, Musée du Louvre, Paris) and lend the painting a romantic air which enhances the appeal of the subject. It has been dated to the late 1840s. In other works Burton presents his sitters in different fashion, **Helen Faucit** (N.G.I. 2359) being represented in classical guise and **Sir Samuel Ferguson** (N.G.I. 2582), the poet and antiquary, being depicted in smart, contemporary dress.

RK

MILDRED ANNE BUTLER, R.W.S.

Kilmurry 1858 - 1941 Kilmurry

*Mildred Anne Butler was born at Kilmurry, a Georgian house near Thomastown, County Kilkenny and spent most of her life living and painting in this peaceful setting. Her father, an army officer, was an amateur artist and probably encouraged his daughter in this occupation. Mildred travelled to France and Switzerland and on into Italy at the age of twenty-seven. In the following years and right up to the outbreak of war she made annual visits to the Continent, and regular trips to London to view the exhibitions. Her first teacher, (apart from the influence of her father), was the Guernsey born landscape painter Paul Jacob Naftel who gently encouraged her to make numerous studies, and to study changing effects of light and sky. She next studied with Frank Calderon who founded the School of Animal Painting in 1894. Her enjoyment and competence with this type of subject matter is evident in her many animal and bird paintings of the 1890s. Mildred spent the summers of 1894 and 1895 in Newlyn where she was taught by Norman Garstin. Garstin and Stanhope Forbes may have introduced her to the Impressionists, their influence is evident also in the new viewpoints she creates in her compositions from chimney tops and angular roofs. Watercolour was her preferred technique, and she concentrated on perfecting her style in that medium. From 1888 she exhibited regularly, notably at the Royal Institute of Painters in Watercolour, the Royal Academy, the Royal Hibernian Academy, the Ulster Academy and the Royal Society of Painters in Watercolour. In 1896 to her delight, she became an Associate of the R.W.S., the same year her painting **The Morning Bath** was purchased for the Tate Gallery. It was not until 1937 that she became a full member of the R.W.S. by which time she was forced by her arthritis to give up painting.*

13 A Preliminary Investigation, 1898

WATERCOLOUR AND GOUACHE ON PAPER 65.5 x 97.5 cms.

SIGNED AND DATED lower left, *Mildred A. Butler 1898*

PROVENANCE By descent from the artist to Mrs Doreen Archer-Houblon, Kilmurry House, Co. Kilkenny; purchased at Christie's, 13 October 1981, lot 47. N.G.I. 7952.

EXHIBITED R.A. 1899 (1116); Kilkenny and Dublin 1981 (41).

LITERATURE Dublin 1982, p. 34, no. 21 (illus.); Le Harivel 1983 p. 43 (illus.); Gillespie, Mooney and Ryan 1986, p.41 (illus.).

Mildred Butler's skill in painting birds was acknowledged first in 1896 when **The Morning Bath,** a picture of pigeons bathing in a fountain, was purchased at the Royal Academy by the Chantrey Bequest for the Tate Gallery. Among her finest and most original works are those which feature birds, and in this she was guided particularly by the animal painter Frank Calderon. The National Gallery of Ireland also possesses the dramatic watercolour of three crows **And straight against that great array went Forth the dauntless Three** (N.G.I. 7958) which was exhibited six years earlier, at the Royal Academy, in 1893.

Encouraged by Calderon she made sketches which were later worked up into a final composition in her studio. A black chalk drawing (Christie's, 10 May 1983, lot 29, 51 x 81 cms.) which relates to **A Preliminary Investigation** is an instance where such a study has survived. In the painting, the artist has divided the picture space diagonally by means of the wooden posts supporting the barn or shed. She has thereby created two triangles confining the action to the lower area of the composition stretching from the upper left to the lower right corner. The background then, comprises the shaded outhouse filled with tools and implements; dull, inanimate objects which contrast with the flock of doves homing in on the spilled sack of corn providing an unexpected mid-day meal. They arrive one after the other with a flurry of wings, their chests puffed up or their heads stretched forward as they investigate their find. Butler evidently studied these birds closely, from every angle; she captures their air of importance and their beady eyed, curious stare. She is confident enough to place one of the doves, viewed from behind, in the foreground. The bright sunshine on the lush green grass and these brilliant white birds, creates an idyllic, rural image. But the great success of this painting is Mildred Butler's technical accomplishment, combining accuracy of drawing with startling light effects.

FC

14 Ancient Rubbish, Kilmurry

WATERCOLOUR ON PAPER 36.5 x 26.4 cms.

PROVENANCE By descent from the artist to Mrs Doreen Archer-Houblon, Kilmurry House, Co. Kilkenny; purchased at Christie's, 13 October 1981, lot 14. N.G.I. 7955

EXHIBITED Kilkenny and Dublin 1981 (6); Dublin 1982 (21).

LITERATURE Le Harivel 1983, p. 44 (illus.).

In *The Athenaeum* of 5 May, 1897 a critic wrote of Butler that 'The young lady knows how to look at her subjects with the eyes of a well-trained artist; she can make good pictures out of simple and indeed trivial material...although there is not a shred of story, anecdote, incident or an atom of pathos...These pictures command attention by the massing and breadth of their chiaroscuro, and the solid way in which they have been handled.'

This is such a scene where the artist paints, quite simply, a corner of her home, Kilmurry. With her back to the window (reflected in the mirror on the left of the back wall), she faces the door, thus opening up the otherwise limited perspective as the viewer's eye is led across the hall and into the far room where the legs of a table can just be made out. The impression she creates is of a comfortable, lived-in family room. The ancient rubbish of the title no doubt refers both to the wicker waste paper basket stuffed with sheets of paper and magazines, and to the jumble of family possessions around it. A sturdy table bears an assortment of books, a candlestick, china tureen, bowl, a vase and a brightly coloured arrangement of anemones. The table is the most clearly defined area of the room, where the light coming from the window behind the artist is reflected in the objects. The back of the chintz covered armchair beyond must hide a fireplace; there appears to be half of a circular firescreen standing against the wall. A large Victorian sideboard with barley-sugar columns occupies the right of the composition, with a barely sketched statue sitting on top. Several small pictures hang on the wall above it, one with a heavy gilt frame. There is a certain awkwardness in the handling of the perspective. The colouring, predominately blues, is most effective; with blue-green walls, a blue carpet, the mauve-blue of the draught excluding curtains on the door, and of the panels in the sideboard. *Ancient Rubbish* may date to the same time as *Kilmurry, an azalea in flower on a table with ornaments before a window* (private collection, signed and dated 1901).

FC

Trained at the Dublin Society School of Architecture, under Henry Aaron Baker, the architect Patrick Byrne received many important commissions following Catholic Emancipation (1829). These included the Franciscan church on Merchant's Quay, known as Adam and Eve's (begun 1830), St Paul's, Arran Quay (1835-37), St Audeon's (begun 1841), and in the suburbs, St Mary's, Rathmines (built 1840s).

15 The Interior of the Royal Exchange, Dublin, 1834

WATERCOLOUR OVER INK ON PAPER 63.5 x 78.5 cms.

SIGNED AND DATED lower left, *Pat.k Byrne 1834;* in margin, lower right, *Patrick Byrne Archt. 1834*

PROVENANCE Purchased from Dr Byrne, 1913. N.G.I. 2688.

EXHIBITED R.H.A. 1861 (568).

LITERATURE Craig 1952, plate 19; Le Harivel 1983, p. 44 (illus.); McParland 1985, plate 41.

The old Tholsel (see Malton, Cat. no. 51) having fallen into poor condition, the merchants of Dublin asked the Wide Street Commissioners to leave a site free for them on Cork Hill. This having been agreed, the merchants purchased the site for £13,500 and began to raise money for a new Exchange. A competition was held and from sixty-one designs a scheme presented by Thomas Cooley was chosen. The competition was held in 1768; the foundation stone was laid on 2 August 1769, and the New Merchants Exchange was complete in 1779. The name was soon altered to the Royal Exchange. In 1852, it became the City Hall. Byrne's view, with its animated official pointing out the features to some visitors, shows the domed interior before the windows were blocked; statues of Charles Lucas, Thomas Drummond and Daniel O'Connell placed around the colonnade and the panels of the frieze painted with scenes of Irish history by James Ward (c.1900).

MW

JOHN HENRY CAMPBELL

Dublin 1757 - 1828 Dublin

Campbell's father came over to Dublin from Herefordshire and was a partner of the King's Printer, Graisbery. His son attended the Dublin Society Schools and exhibited views of Dublin and County Wicklow, with an occasional portrait or scene of smugglers, from 1800-19, and at two R.H.A. exhibitions 1826 and 1828. Moonlight scenes, no doubt showing a similar romanticism to his few sombre oils, were also shown.

16 The river Dargle near Enniskerry, County Wicklow

WATERCOLOUR ON PAPER 37.2 x 37.4 cms.

INSCRIBED on verso, *View up the River at Enniskerry, Co. Wicklow 10 Miles from Dublin - Shank Hill in the Distance*

PROVENANCE Pakenham Mahon family, Strokestown, Co. Roscommon; presented to Mrs Waistell at an unknown date and purchased from her son, Captain Alan M. Waistell, Hereford, 1939. N.G.I. 6344.

LITERATURE Le Harivel 1983, p. 48 (illus.).

Like other landscapists of this era, Campbell often painted the wooded landscape around the Powerscourt Estate in County Wicklow, and along the river Dargle. The inscription on the *verso* suggests that this is the adjacent Glencullen river, which flows from the hills down to the village of Enniskerry (then as now much visited by tourists) joining the river Dargle near Bray and the awesome Glen of the Dargle. The distant peak is however the more distinguished Great Sugar Loaf (1,654 ft.), equally visible from Enniskerry and a constant motif in views of Wicklow. Campbell exhibited a view of *Shankhill, from Fassero, Co. Wicklow* at the Society of Artists of Ireland in 1811. While Campbell may seem to create an idyllic rustic scene with contented farmer and neat cottage, in fact this area of Ireland was prosperous, and the single-storey thatched cottages typical of the time. His repoussoir tree framing the view on the right is very much part of the classical landscape tradition and continues the elegant world of T.S. Roberts into the 19th century. Campbell's figure painting is less assured, as in the strangely jointed woman at work by the cottage. Campbell works without pencil and landscape details tend to merge in a dense blue-green colouring. Foliage is picked out in large shapes. This watercolour, and five others in the collection, once belonged to the Packenham Mahon family of Strokestown House, County Roscommon. They lived there from 1649-1979, witnessing the glamour of Georgian Ireland and the horror of the famine years.

ALH

HARRY CLARKE, R.H.A.

Dublin 1889 - 1931 Coire

Having attended school at Belvedere College until he was 14, Clarke assisted his father in the family stained glass business on North Frederick Street. He won a scholarship to study stained glass under Alfred Ernest Child at the Metropolitan School of Art 1911-13 and visited France, particularly Chartres Cathedral, in 1914. From 1915-17 he made eleven windows for the Honan Chapel, Cork which established him with his distinctive style. He also made a series of literary illustrations on glass up to 1921. He then took over the family business, which soon expanded to employ twenty-seven assistants. By 1925, he had completed his finest work, over forty commissions for Ireland and Britain, also secular masterpieces **The Eve of St. Agnes** (Hugh Lane Municipal Gallery of Modern Art) and **The Geneva Window** (Mitchell Wolfson Museum, Miami). Clarke exhibited at the Irish Arts and Crafts Society and illustrated a number of books in the 1920s. He suffered from ill-health, and from 1926, enlarged photographs of his designs were used as cartoons by the Studios, in order to delegate work further. In spite of a near fatal accident that year, he took on more work and died of consumption in a Swiss Sanitorium in 1931. The Studios continued to make glass, in his style, until 1973.

17 'See Fierce Belinda on the Baron Flies' (Pope), 1913

INK OVER PENCIL ON CARD 37 x 28 (image 28 x 15) cms.

SIGNED AND DATED upper right, and on *verso*, Harry Clarke 1913

INSCRIBED ON MOUNT in gothic script, *See Fierce Belinda on the Baron flies, With more than usual lightning in her eyes: "The Rape of the Lock" Pope.*

PROVENANCE Commissioned by Laurence Ambrose Waldron 1913; bequeathed to his niece, Cicily O'Kelly, 1923, from whom purchased 1936. N.G.I. 2960.

LITERATURE Le Harivel 1983, p. 58 (illus.); Bowe 1983, pp. 12, 108-11 (illus.); Bowe 1989, pp. 28-29.

This is one of six illustrations to Alexander Pope's 1714 comic poem **The Rape of the Lock** (N.G.I. 2957-2962). It was a private commission and never published. The story, set at Hampton Court, where 'Great Anna...Dost sometimes counsel take - and sometimes tea' (Canto 1), concerns the theft by the Baron of a lock of Belinda's hair. Here she turns on the Baron as he begs forgiveness, and prepares to throw snuff and wound him with her bodkin (later a treasured possession in the Baron's family). Eventually sylphs place the lock in the firmament. Pope was inspired by a real incident where Lord Petre cut off a lock of Miss Arabella Fermor's hair, but his style parodies the story of the Rape of Helen and siege of Troy, with frequent quotations from Homer and Virgil. He also attacks her pride for 'beauty must decay...locks will turn to grey...And she who scorns a man, must die a maid' (Canto 5). Clarke responds to the affected behaviour of the characters in the poem using the fussy clothes of the Baron to suggest his egotism, while the stiffly arranged hair of Belinda and the barrier formed by her black dress express her haughty character. He was well aware that Aubrey Beardsley had illustrated the poem in 1896. Clarke chose the same scenes, but in this early work he is not as skillful in his delineation of figures, or treatment of space. He borrows techniques of cross hatching and fine dotted work. As in literary stained glass designs of the period such as **The Mad Prince** (N.G.I. 12,074) his brilliance is seen in the balance of hard outline and intricate surface decoration. Clarke's initial underdrawing in pencil can still be seen on the table ornaments and he had established the regular floor pattern before realising more space was needed for Belinda's crinolined skirt. **The Rape of the Lock** was commissioned by Laurence Waldron, a Governor of Belvedere College, who was an important patron of Clarke from 1912 until the artist's death. He also introduced him to a lively milieu at his Killiney home, where Clarke met many future patrons.

ALH

18 Two textile designs for Sefton Fabrics, Belfast, 1919

a) WATERCOLOUR OVER INK ON PAPER 23.6 x 18 cms.

SIGNED on *verso, H C*

b) WATERCOLOUR OVER PENCIL ON PAPER 8.5 x 10.5 cms.

SIGNED centre right, *H C*

PROVENANCE Bequeathed to artist's son, David Clarke, from whom purchased, through The Taylor Galleries Ltd., Dublin, 1982. N.G.I. 7962; 7965.

EXHIBITED Dublin 1979 (134); Dublin 1982 (30).

LITERATURE Le Harivel 1983, p. 60 (illus.); Bowe 1989, pp. 94, 96-97.

Clarke was commissioned in December 1918 by Walter Sefton, of Sefton Fabrics, Ormeau Avenue, Belfast, to design a set of eight silk handkerchiefs, and some dress fabrics for their **Sherevoile** range. The handkerchiefs were printed in 1919. There are four unused designs in the collection of which two are shown here. The other two are an **Arabesque** in red (N.G.I. 7963) and a **Check Pattern** (N.G.I. 7964). The large **Butterfly design** here in suffuse pinks, purples and lime greens is an intricate pattern of sea urchin and butterflies set among tendrils and flowerbuds, on a pale blue ground. The complexity and lack of easily read symmetry, suggests why it was not chosen for reproduction. The other is a **Floral design** with ink outline and colouring in yellow and pink. It is shown with the signature upside down, so the patterns of floral displays and leaf patterns make sense. It recalls printed cottons by William Morris, though Clarke has evolved from the strict repetition of 19th century Arts and Crafts designs. A second set of eight handkerchiefs was made in 1920. Late 1918 was a productive time for Clarke, when he was also engaged on illustrations to Edgar Allan Poe's **Tales of Mystery and Imagination,** windows for five churches, projected reproductions of glass panels and his own Christmas card.

ALH

From 1748 Dixon was established as a picture dealer in Capel Street, Dublin, from where he also later sold Flower Pieces of the type here exhibited. He employed apprentices to colour his designs - including the future miniature painters Gustavus Hamilton, James Reilly and Daniel O'Keefe.

19 A Bull-Finch and Blue Tit-Mouse, with peaches and apricots, c.1755

GOUACHE AND WATERCOLOUR ON EMBOSSED PAPER 30.8 x 40.4 cms.

DEDICATED ON FRAME REVERSE to the Countess Dowager Kildare (sic) on printed label

PROVENANCE Marquesses of Hastings, Donnington Hall; by descent to Loudoun Castle, Ayr; McTears Auction Rooms, Glasgow, 7 November 1930; purchased at Sotheby's, 19 March, 1982, lot 12A. N.G.I. 18,298.

EXHIBITED Dublin 1982 (33).

LITERATURE Longfield 1975, p. 131; Le Harivel 1983, p. 104 (illus.).

Dixon is mostly associated with this type of embossed picture. The compositions were coloured by Dixon himself and by artists whom he employed. The latter sometimes signed them. Birds and flowers were Dixon's main subjects. Frequently, as here, these embossed watercolours were inserted in black and gold japanned frames which add to their highly decorative quality.

Dixon issued three sets of these embossed pictures and, from the outset, claimed that the technique was his invention. The first set of twelve was issued in 1748, and the subjects were delightful groups of flowers. The success of this venture caused him to proceed with a second set of twelve pictures, available from 1750. These were of foreign birds, based directly on plates from George Edwards's *Natural History of Uncommon Birds,* which was published in several volumes from 1743 onwards. Their popularity was sufficient to produce at least one 'pirate' and in an effort to circumvent the potential danger to Dixon's reputation, the 1750 set was dedicated to the Earl of Meath. A third set of foreign and domestic birds, again numbering twelve, was available from 1755, and each of these was dedicated to a notable person, with a description of the subject, all printed on elegant labels affixed to the reverse of the picture, in order to ensure authenticity. The work exhibited here comes from this third set of successful and charmingly artistic works of art and may be dated to about 1755. The former owners of this watercolour were the Hastings family. The mother of the future 1st Marquess married the Earl of Moira in Dublin providing an Irish link.

MW

RICHARD DOYLE

London 1824 - 1883 London

Richard ('Dicky') Doyle was the second son of political cartoonist John Doyle ('HB'), (1797-1868). He grew up in an enclosed family world, with a private tutor and drawing lessons from his father. Both his brothers Henry Doyle (1826-1892) and Charles Doyle (1832-1893) were later artists. The author Sir Arthur Conan Doyle was his nephew. Doyle's whimsical view of life and history, both comic and fantastic, is seen from an early age in 'Nonsense sketchbooks' and his first publication the **Comical procession of Remarkable Personages** (1842). From 1842-50, he was a regular contributor of cartoons and comic borders to **Punch,** and his cover design was used to this century. He left due to attacks on the Roman Catholic church in editorials and cartoons. Illustrations for **The Fairy Ring** (1846) by the Grimm Brothers had already established him as a leading fairy painter, with **In Fairyland** (1870), his printed masterpiece, though he painted fairy subjects throughout his life. Doyle's talent for humorous observation is well seen in **The Manners and Customs of the English** (1849) and **The Foreign Tour of Messrs. Brown, Jones and Robinson** (1854). From 1850-70 he illustrated books by Thackeray (a close friend), Dickens, Ruskin and others, after when he mainly painted watercolours. There was a major exhibition of his work at the Grosvenor Gallery in 1881. He died suddenly two years later.

20 A mother, child and dog, 1870s

WATERCOLOUR OVER PENCIL ON PAPER 17.6 x 30.5 cms.

PROVENANCE Purchased at Richard Doyle sale, Christie's, 7 June 1866. N.G.I. 3301.

LITERATURE Le Harivel 1983, p. 116 (illus.).

When not painting fantasy subjects or observing society's foibles, Doyle found great pleasure in recording the world around him. Here, a watchful mother restrains her son from running after the family dog by gently tugging on his sash. The child is very young and has not graduated to male clothes. It is the most finished of five watercolours in the collection bought by his brother Henry Doyle (then Director of the National Gallery of Ireland) at Doyle's posthumous sale, where they were described as **Mothers and children.** In each, the child is held, or beckoned to, by its Mother (or possibly Nanny), and they evoke a secure world of untroubled childhood, much as Walter Osborne captures in his work (Cat. no. 60). The woman is informally dressed, without even wearing a cap. An Elizabethan house is glimpsed beyond an oak tree. The same figures may be shown in N.G.I. 3313 and the woman in N.G.I. 3314. The clothes indicate a date in the 1870s. The theme is made more poignant by the knowledge that Doyle's own mother died when he was eight and that he had a very regimented childhood. In **Dick's Journal of 1840** (British Museum) he emphasises the more amusing domestic incidents, but also shows himself alone in bed, surrounded by the fairies which already filled his imagination. John Doyle's practice of sending his children to sketch London life trained him to quickly note down essentials, here establishing strong outlines to the figures, then filling in clothes and the copse behind, with small, closely spaced, strokes of colour.

ALH

GEORGE VICTOR DU NOYER

Dublin 1817 - 1869 Antrim

The son of a French music teacher from Marseilles, who had married into a Dublin Huguenot family, Du Noyer studied painting under George Petrie. Aged twenty, he became a draughtsman with the Ordnance Survey, a very advanced body technologically in those days. Working with this institution he became very interested in Irish antiquities, to which he would have been introduced at an early stage by his master Petrie.

*Du Noyer transferred to the Geological Survey of Ireland, and it was while working with them in the field that he contracted scarlet fever, from which he died. Eighteen of his drawings were used to illustrate Hall's **Ireland, its scenery, character etc.** (1841-43) and he lithographed himself his frontispiece for Burton's **History of the Royal Hospital, Kilmainham** (1843). In addition, a large corpus of bound drawings and watercolours are in the Royal Irish Academy.*

21 Dunmoe Castle, County Meath, 1844

WATERCOLOUR ON PAPER 39.1 x 48.4 cms.

SIGNED lower right, *Geo: du Noyer. Delt. 1844*

INSCRIBED on old backing paper, probably the original, *Dunmoe Castle. on the Boyne Co. Meath April 1844. Geo: Du Noyer;* lower right, 156-95 (National Museum of Ireland inventory number)

PROVENANCE Royal Dublin Society; acquired by the State 1877 and lodged in the National Museum of Ireland until transferred in 1966. N.G.I. 3980.

LITERATURE McGoogan 1915, p. 21, no. 26 (illus. opp. p. 20); Le Harivel 1983, p. 121 (illus.); de Courcy and Maher 1985, p. 26 (illus.).

Dunmoe Castle, overlooking the river Boyne between Slane and Navan, but closer to the latter, was orignally four-storied with large rounded turrets at each corner. Though thirteenth century in style, it was probably not built until the fifteenth century (Harbison 1970, pp. 183-84).

Dunmoe Castle was the subject of engravings, the most interesting of which is that in Francis Grose's, ***The Antiquities of Ireland*** (London 1791-95), vol. 2, plate 65. By the time Du Noyer visited it, the castle was in a poor state of repair. He was then teaching art at St Columba's College, which may explain why it is unusually well finished, with fine detail in the trees and men in the fields. The brightly lit sweep of the riverbank gives an unexpected grandeur to the ruins beyond, which are in shadow as rain clouds pass overhead.

MW

JOHN FAULKNER, R.H.A.

fl. Dublin 1848 - 1890 *London*

Nothing is known of Faulkner's parents. He attended the Royal Dublin Society Schools from 1848-52 and exhibited oil and watercolour landscapes at the Royal Hibernian Academy from 1853. Views of County Wicklow dominate in the 1850s, with Scottish subjects appearing from 1861, the year he was elected an Associate R.H.A. In 1862 he became a full Member. Faulkner led an irregular life and his departure from Dublin in 1870 was coupled with explusion from the R.H.A., for unspecified reasons. Having visited America, he settled in London and exhibited 1887-90 at the Royal Academy and at the Royal Scottish Academy. From 1880-87 he sent landscapes of County Mayo, Warwick and Coblenz to the R.H.A., but there is no later record of him.

22 A Burn at Glenfinnan, Argyleshire, c.1888

WATERCOLOUR OVER CHARCOAL ON PAPER 76.1 x 125.7 cms.

SIGNED lower left, *John Faulkner*

INSCRIBED lower right, *A Burn at Glenfinnan, Argyleshire*

PAPER WATERMARKED *James Whatman Turkey Mill Kent 1888*

PROVENANCE Purchased at Bearne's, Torquay, 3 November 1982, lot 167. N.G.I. 19,182.

EXHIBITED Dublin 1983 (32).

LITERATURE Le Harivel 1983, p. 143 (illus.); Gillespie, Mooney and Ryan 1985, p. 37 (illus.).

Glenfinnan, by Loch Shiel in the Western Highlands, is judged one of the most beautiful areas in this part of Scotland. Victorian tourists visited it also for historical associations, to see the monument (erected in 1815) where on 19 August 1745 the Marquess of Tullibardine raised the Standard of Prince Charles Edward Stewart (Bonnie Prince Charlie) to rally the clans and retake the English throne. Two days later the Prince began his ill-fated march on London with eventual defeat at Culloden. In Faulkner's watercolour, the peaks in the distance are above the unseen Loch, and our viewpoint is the river Finnan, which flows into it from the north. The poet, Sir Walter Scott, was the first to promote natural Scottish scenery, ruins, and places of historic interest as worthy of being written about and painted. Queen Victoria was an enthusiast for wild and sublime Scottish features which engendered a sense of solitude, while in 1847 a leading cultural figure, Lady Eastlake, praised 'every inch of a burn, with ferns hanging over it, and every stone, round which it ripples, rich in colour' (Eastlake 1895, p. 210). This perception of landscape, allied to Ruskin's belief in fidelity to nature and precise, scientific drawing partly explain the popularity of such views in Victorian art. Faulkner's vision is perhaps more romantic, with a rich palette from ochre to purple, the frisson of spray against the rocks, and with his low viewpoint, a sense of total isolation. The influence of Turner and Varley are seen in the colours and techniques of scraping and spongeing, while the size reflects the greater esteem given to watercolour painting in the 19th century. His oil landscapes tend to be less dramatic.

ALH

THOMAS FRYE

c. Dublin 1710 · 1762 London

Born possibly at Edenderry, County Offaly,
nothing is known of Frye's early life. He was in
London by 1736 when he received a very
important commission from the Saddlers'
Company to portray, in full length, Frederick
Prince of Wales. This large picture was
destroyed during World War II, but an idea of
its grandeur may be obtained by looking at the
engraving of it; additionally, a less formal, but
very competent half-length of the same sitter
remains in the Royal Collection to this day. Frye
was clearly a very successful painter, to judge
by the number of works which survive. One of
the most beautiful must surely be that of **Mrs
Wardle,** who wears sumptuous clothes, which
was purchased by the Yale Center for British Art
at New Haven, a few years ago. In 1744, Frye
was a co-founder of the Bow porcelain factory,
and its first manager. There are some grounds
to believe that he had some influence in the
designs of some of the factory's earliest
products (Wynne 1982, p. 624). Frye had a
decided influence on at least two artists, the
not very well-known Irish pastellist, Robert
Healy and one of England's really major
eighteenth century painters, Joseph Wright of
Derby. Before engaging in the Bow enterprise,
Frye executed some fine mezzotints. In 1760 he
became ill. He went to Wales for the benfit of
his health and then returned to London. In the
next two years he scraped two series of
mezzotints, fanciful heads, which print experts
acknowledge to be among the most
accomplished works in that technique.
Advowedly indebted to Piazzetta, it was these
mezzotints that made such an impact on Wright
of Derby.

23 Portrait of an Artist

BLACK AND WHITE CHALK ON BLUE PAPER 42.4 x 30.8 cms.

PROVENANCE Purchased from Tregaskis, London, 1907. N.G.I. 2634.

EXHIBITED London and New York 1967 (59).

LITERATURE White 1967, pp. 411-412; Wynne 1972, p. 84, no. 42, fig. 26; Le Harivel 1983, p. 176 (illus.).

To date it has not been possible to identify the artist seen here at work on a drawing. Frye imbues his sitters with a strong feeling of intensity. In this sheet Frye used fewer fine stroke lines than usual, creating effect with more stump. However, it would be imprudent to generalise too much since autograph Frye drawings, some of which relate to his mezzotints, are not numerous.

MW

WILHELMINA MARGARET GEDDES

Drumreilly 1887 · 1955 London

Born at Drumreilly, in County Leitrim, where her father was a site engineer on the railway, the family soon moved to Belfast. After Methodist College, she transferred, at the age of sixteen, to the Belfast Art School, where she was awarded many prizes. From 1910 she attended William Orpen's classes at the Metropolitan School of Art in Dublin. At the studio of **An Túr Gloine** in 1911, she made three small panels illustrating the story of Saint Colman MacDuagh (Hugh Lane Municipal Gallery of Modern Art, Dublin), which made a great impression on Sarah Purser, a founder of the studio. Already in these early small works one can detect the immense power in line, colour and structure, which came to characterise her later full scale windows. In 1918 she designed three windows depicting Archangels for All Saints Church, Blackrock, County Dublin. Sadly one was destroyed by a fire, the second, damaged, may be seen in the porch, while the third, Archangel Michael, remains intact. Here one may appreciate Geddes's full power, and a strong individuality of expression. Following a long illness, Geddes formally left **An Túr Gloine,** in 1922. A couple of years later she established herself in a studio in the Fulham Glass House, from which, despite intermittent illness, she completed some of her most important commissions, several of which were forwarded to her by Sarah Purser. Here she was able to be as individual as she pleased, untrammelled. She is one of the greatest European stained glass artists of the first half of the twentieth century.

24 Warrior Saints and Archangels outside Sion, c.1919

WATERCOLOUR OVER INK AND PENCIL ON PAPER 38.0 x 30.5 cms.

PROVENANCE *An Túr Gloine* studio; presented by Patrick Pollen, Dublin 1966. N.G.I. 18,434.

EXHIBITED Edinburgh 1985 (72).

LITERATURE Le Harivel 1983, p. 180 (illus.); Bowe 1987, pp. 57-58; Bowe, Caron and Wynne 1988, p. 80.

This sketch design is for a stained glass window, commissioned by HRH The Duke of Connaught and Strathearn, as a war memorial to officers of his Canadian staff, in the Governor General's (St Bartholomew's) Chapel, Government Buildings, Ottawa, Canada. Warrior saints and Angels greet a fallen soldier outside the walls of Sion. The commission came to **An Túr Gloine** studio in 1917, and was entrusted to Geddes. The window, completed in 1919, varies in many details from both this design and an earlier one (N.G.I. 18,433). As completed, St Michael is shown full-face, the lion is omitted, the lower lights have figures. The history of the window can be followed in letters to her niece (unpublished).

Prince Arthur William Albert, Duke of Connaught and Strathearn (1850-1942) was the third son of Queen Victoria and visited Dublin as a boy (see Mahony, Cat. no. 50). He became a career soldier, trained and commissioned at Woolwich as a Royal Engineer. In 1869 he was sent to Montreal for a year. As a royal prince he was given special assignments, but his principal interest was in his profession. He saw action in North Africa, India and elsewhere. In 1911 he was appointed Governor-general of Canada, a post which he enjoyed until 1918, when he retired.

MW

GEORGE GRATTAN

Dublin 1787 - 1819 Dublin

Grattan showed great promise at the Dublin Society Schools where he painted miniatures and received drawing prizes from 1797-1803, having already exhibited portraits and landscapes at the Parliament House in 1801. In 1803, though General Vallancey, he carried out some landscapes and pastel portraits for the Lord Lieutenant, Earl Hardwicke. In 1804, having left the Schools, he exhibited chiefly views from Counties Dublin and Wicklow, and soon began to establish himself as an oil painter too. The poignant **Blind beggarwoman and child** (1807) was bought by the Dublin Society and even its carriage to exhibition in London paid for. It was his sole Dublin exhibit in 1809, the year he failed to supplant the West family and become Master of the Dublin Society School. Following his complaints, the Dublin Society purchased his test drawings. From 1801-13 Grattan exhibited historical scenes and genre at the Royal Academy, visiting London 1812-13. Ill-health seems to have ended his career and he never exhibited again. His brother William (c.1792 - after 1825) arranged a posthumous showing of seventy-five pictures and drawings and himself exhibited landscapes in Dublin from 1809-15.

25 The Guard Room, 1811

WATERCOLOUR ON PAPER 45.1 x 55.7 cms.

SIGNED bottom centre, G. Grattan pinx 1811

PROVENANCE Unknown. N.G.I. 7380.

EXHIBITED R.A. 1812 (539); Dublin 1813 (67).

LITERATURE Strickland 1913, vol. I, pp. 406-07. Le Harivel 1983, p. 185 (illus.).

The scene illustrates Canto 6 of Sir Walter Scott's **Lady of the Lake,** an epic poem published in 1810 and dedicated to the Marquess of Abercorn. Set around Loch Katrine, each Canto lasting a day, it concerns the plight of Ellen, daughter of the outlawed Lord Douglas. Three suitors wish to marry her (one is the King in disguise). She has come secretly to Stirling Castle, to beg the King to pardon her father, but even at the door, as she arrives hidden 'in plaid/All muffled close, a mountain maid', John of Brent challenges, Bertram, one of her companions, to a fight.

'But Ellen boldly stepp'd between
And dropp'd at once the tartan screen;
So, from his morning cloud, appears
The sun of May through summer tears'.

The picture was exhibited with this quotation from Canto 6. Although the whole Canto is titled '**The Guard Room**', Grattan has chosen one of the more dramatic moments, with the statuesque Ellen, standing out against a harper in plaid and 'grey and scarred' Bertram, as she faces John of Brent. In an inner room, the King's soldiers lie in a drunken stupour or carouse around the fire. The story ends with the King and Lord Douglas reconciled, the evil Roderick dead and Ellen married to Malcolm Graeme. Scott's poem, with its scenic Scottish locations and stirring drama, was frequently illustrated by artists at the time. Grattan exhibited **The Gathering** (from Canto 3) in both London and Dublin. He creates a sense of grandeur, even on a small scale, in the tradition of Irish subject painters like Henry Brooke and James Barry. Much of the work is in a brownish tone, without underdrawing, and the main figures stand out in stronger colours. The room is a curious mixture of medieval and classical architecture, the costume detail equally imaginative.

ALH

NATHANIEL GROGAN

Cork c.1740 - 1807 *Cork*

Grogan was apprenticed to his father, a turner and block maker. Unhappy in this calling, he ran away to sea. He served in America and the West Indies. Returning to Cork he embarked on an artistic career. His works fall into two principal categories, landscapes and genre scenes, the latter verging on caricature at times. In addition he executed many engravings, his twelve views of Cork, in aquatint, being particularly fine.

26 Figures seated below a ruined castle

INK WITH BLUE AND GREY WASHES ON PAPER **34 x 48.4 cms.**

PROVENANCE Unknown. N.G.I. 7422.

LITERATURE Le Harivel 1983, p. 188 (illus.); Gillespie, Mooney and Ryan 1986, p. 6 (illus.).

Grogan liked to work from known sites and prospects; in this case, however, the ruins are so elaborate that we are almost certainly confronted with an Irish capriccio. The fluid brush-strokes and washes are typical of Grogan's style.

A beautiful example of a Grogan watercolour of a known place is that of Blarney Castle, County Cork, and the old bridge nearby (Richard Wood Collection at Fota House, near Cork). The figures in Grogan's topographical work are invariably well drawn and frequently more elegantly dressed than their respective occupations would suggest.

MW

JACK P. HANLON

Templeogue 1913 - 1968 *Dublin*

John Thomas Hanlon was educated by the Jesuits at Belvedere College, Dublin. Art was not part of the school curriculum and he received art lessons outside school time. In 1932 on completion of his secondary education he entered Clonliffe College to study for the priesthood, was ordained in 1939 and served in several Dublin parishes. While at college he continued his art studies, at the Ablett Studios, although it can not have been easy to devote as much time as he might have liked to this pursuit, and he passed the examination of the Royal Drawing Society. His friendship with Mainie Jellett was to prove a key influence in his development as an artist. He became her pupil in the late 1930s. Jellett had studied in Paris with André Lhote and Albert Gleizes, and with Evie Hone brought Cubism to Ireland. Later, Hanlon himself went to Paris to study with Lhote, possibly spending up to eighteen months there in the time between his ordination and his first clerical post. While Lhote's Cubist approach and techniques had a profound and lasting influence on his work, Hanlon was also drawn to the work of the Fauves in Paris, the bright colours of his watercolours being inspired by Mediterranean sunshine rather than the Irish climate.

He was a founder member of the Irish Exhibition of Living Art, remaining a committee member until his death in 1968. He painted prolifically, and had numerous one-man shows in Dublin, London, Paris and Brussels, his work also represented in exhibitions of contemporary Irish Art abroad. He was the recipient of a number of prizes including the Hallmark International Art Award (1955), and the Douglas Hyde Gold Medal And Arts Council Prize (1962).

27 Fiery Leaves

WATERCOLOUR ON PAPER **66.5 x 49 cms.**

SIGNED **lower right,** *JACK P HANLON*

PROVENANCE **Bequeathed by the artist, 1968. N.G.I. 6888.**

LITERATURE **Le Harivel 1983, p. 234 (illus.); Butler 1990, p. 97, fig. 98.**

Jack Hanlon bequeathed six sheets and fifty-five sketch books to the National Gallery of Ireland. The highly finished watercolours and drawings are thought to date from 1935-38, in contrast to the later period from the 1940s to 1960s, when his approach becomes freer, and more decorative. The influence of the Fauves with their feeling for flat pattern and bright colours is clear in *Fiery Leaves.* The curved outline of the vase is treated simply as an essential prop for the explosion of colour and shapes which fill the composition, their bright, dilute colour, balanced by unpainted areas of paper.

FC

EDWARD HAYES, R.H.A.

County Tipperary 1797 - 1864 Dublin

Little is known of his early years, when he studied at the Dublin Society Schools and also c.1812 with J.S. Alpenny (see Cat. no. 1). He painted miniatures in Clonmel, Kilkenny and Waterford and later stated he had taught drawing at the Abbeyleix Institute, Kilkenny College and the Ursuline Convent, Waterford. In 1830 he sent still-life, oil landscapes and a self-portrait to the R.H.A. from Waterford, and in 1832 moved to 37 College Green, Dublin, advertising himself as a miniature painter. He exhibited mainly portraits at the R.H.A. until 1864, also landscapes of Counties Tipperary, Waterford and Wicklow, with an occasional subject piece. Hayes was elected an Associate of the R.H.A. in 1856 and full member 1861. His son was Michael Angelo Hayes.

28 The Choir Doorway, Athassel Priory, County Tipperary, c.1861

WATERCOLOUR ON PAPER 46.4 x 56 cms.

SIGNED lower right, *Edwd. Hayes R.H.A.*

PROVENANCE Presented by Miss Geoghegan, Sandycove, 1923. N.G.I. 2728.

EXHIBITED ?1861 R.H.A. (387); 1980 Dublin (38).

LITERATURE Le Harivel 1983, p. 244 (illus.); de Courcy and Maher 1986, p. 45 (illus.).

The splayed doorway (c.1260), with foliage capitals and dogtooth ornament, leading from the nave to the choir in Athassel Priory, is the most impressive feature of the medieval Priory. The shallow arched recess above is thought to have once held a great Crucifix and statuary, forming a Rood Screen. It was filled in to support the crossing tower when rebuilt soon after nobles devastated and burnt the Priory in 1447, leaving the nave roofless. The East windows seen here also date from the fifteenth century. Athassel Priory was an Augustinian order, founded under the protection of William FitzAdelm de Burgo (d.1205) on the west bank of the river Suir. His son and grandson are both buried there. The Priory covers nearly four acres, with extensive cloistral buildings, but is now completely roofless, with no trace of the town which grew up adjacent to it and was twice burnt in the fourteenth century. In Hayes's day the choir doorway was half sunken in the ground, ivy clung to the stonework and there was a tree growing in the choir. There is a similar view in Hall's *Ireland, its scenery, character, etc.* (1841-43, vol. 2, p. 95) and a vignette from further away shows trees also growing in the nave (p. 94). Athassel Priory had not been much visited by 18th century Antiquarians and was not included in Grose's *The Antiquities of Ireland* (1791-95). The visitor in Hayes's view is a serious traveller with bowler hat, overcoat, cape and staff. The watercolour dates from c.1861 when Hayes exhibited other views of County Tipperary, and is one of his most accomplished works.

ALH

MICHAEL ANGELO HAYES

Waterford 1820 - 1877 *Dublin*

He was the son of Edward Hayes, who trained him. His principal interests were equine and military subjects, with similar themes as treated by artists such as Lady Butler and Edouard Detaille. While still a boy, entrepreneur Charles Bianconi had his drawings of **Car-travelling in the South of Ireland in the year 1836** *published in London by Ackerman (re-issued 1856, N.G.I. 20, 695-20, 700) and Hayes exhibited his first military subject at the R.H.A. in 1837. He was created Military Painter-in-Ordinary to the Lord Lieutenant in 1842 and his illustrations to the ballad* **Savourneen Deelish** *received a prize from the Royal Irish Art Union, and were lithographed, in 1846. He is next found in London, where he exhibited once at the Royal Academy in 1848 and was elected an Associate of the Society of Painters in Watercolours the same year. Returning to Dublin in 1853, he was elected an Associate of the R.H.A., a Member in 1854 and Secretary in 1856. He became embroiled in the schism of 1856, when he was replaced the following year by Mulrenin and Martin Cregan, as President , by George Petrie. Following the granting of a new charter in 1860, Hayes returned and was re-elected Secretary from 1861-70. He continued to exhibit until 1874.*

29 Sackville Street, Dublin, c.1853

WATERCOLOUR OVER PENCIL, WITH GUM ARABIC AND WHITE HIGHLIGHTS ON PAPER 54.5 x 77.6 cms.

SIGNED lower right, *M Angelo Hayes R. H. A.*

LITHOGRAPHED BY W. Simpson, published Day and Son, London.

PROVENANCE Purchased from Mrs L. Meade, Dublin, 1942. N.G.I. 2980.

EXHIBITED R.H.A. 1854 (190); O.W.S. 1858; Dallas 1976 (48); Dublin 1988(-).

LITERATURE Strickland 1913, vol. I, p. 465; Le Harivel 1983, p. 245 (illus.); de Courcy and Maher 1985, p. 16 (illus.).

Sackville Street, renamed O'Connell Street in 1930, has long been the central thoroughfare of Dublin. The view here shows the portico of the General Post Office, the distant spire of St George's, Hardwicke Place; the Nelson Pillar, and the Imperial Hotel. In the early 18th century this was Drogheda Street, but land developer Luke Gardiner widened it c.1750 to its present 150 feet, as an enclosed Mall of houses with central area for promenading. It was renamed Sackville Street in 1756 after Lord Sackville, Lord Lieutenant from 1751-55. In the 1790s the street was linked to College Green and the south of the city by the Wide Street Commissioners over Carlisle (now O'Connell) bridge. The only original house is near the top, beyond the General Post Office, which was designed by Francis Johnston (1814-18) and rebuilt inside after the siege and bombardment of the 1916 Easter Rising. The Greek Ionic portico of Portland stone has statues of Fidelity, Hibernia and Mercury by Thomas Kirk. Nelson Pillar, designed by William Wilkins (1808), was the first column to commemorate Admiral Lord Nelson. Over 134 feet high, it was crowned by Thomas Kirk's 13 feet statue of Nelson, set on a podium with the names of his four great victories. A focal point of Dublin, omnibuses ran to the Pillar, even after it was blown up and had to be demolished in 1966. Nelson's head survives in the Civic Museum. The Imperial Hotel is next to the store of McSwiney, Delany and Co. designed by William Deane Butler in 1853. Its prominence in this view owes much to Peter McSwiney being the brother-in-law of the artist. Mahony also served as his Secretary when he became Lord Mayor. The business was acquired in 1884 by Clery's, whose present store dates from 1919-22. Next door, Mahony shows the old facade of the textile merchant Richard Allen's shop, which was rebuilt 1850-53 with a gallery and caryatids. The view is also fascinating for its glimpse of 1850s Dublin life: shoppers, a policeman, tradesman's boy, mother and child, various carriages and carts and even the No. 2 omnibus from Portobello. Mahony had a particular interest in recording moving animals. He published an illustrated pamphlet *The Delineation of Animals in rapid motion* in 1876.

ALH

MICHAEL HEALY

Dublin 1873 · 1941 Dublin

*A Dubliner, Michael Healy was born into a
family of modest circumstances. He did not
attend art classes until he was aged twenty-four
when he enrolled at the Metropolitan School of
Art, and he later attended the Royal Hibernian
Academy Schools. Under the patronage of
Father Glendon, OP, he went to Italy in 1899
for eighteen months, working mainly in
Florence. Upon his return, he became art
master at the Dominican Fathers' College in
Newbridge, County Kildare.*

*On the strength of his exhibited and published
work, he was invited to join **An Túr Gloine,** at
its foundation in 1903. He was a trained artist,
but one who had to learn the art and craft of
the stained glass medium. This he absorbed
from the founder-manager of the studio, Alfred
Ernest Child. Healy clearly relished this new
medium, and after a number of years he was
producing windows in rich deep colours,
embarking on the use of aciding to accentuate
the hieratic quality of appropriate passages,
and even entire windows. Needless to say, his
draughtsmanship was superb, and as he
developed his own stained glass idiom, the
lines became more simplified and stronger,
counterpointing the lead lines. Healy remained
at the studio until his death in 1941, producing
an abundant quantity of quality work. In his
leisure time he sketched incessantly, in pencil
and in watercolour.*

30 St Patrick lighting the Paschal Fire on the Hill of Slane, c.1914

WATERCOLOUR OVER INK AND PENCIL ON PAPER 27.2 x 28 cms.

PROVENANCE *An Túr Gloine* studio; presented by Mr Patrick Pollen, Dublin, 1966.
N.G.I. 18,363.

LITERATURE Le Harivel 1983, p. 268 (illus.); Bowe, Caron and Wynne 1988, pp. 51
and 86.

This is a sketch design for a cinquefoil panel which was executed in stained glass
for the apex of a two-light window in the Catholic Church at Donnybrook,
Dublin and separately for the Cranbrook Academy of Art Museum, Bloomfield
Hills, Michigan, USA (Bowe 1990-91, p. 181, illus.).

The Hill of Slane rises high above, and north of, the river Boyne, in County
Meath. Accounts of early Christianity in Ireland narrate how on this hill St
Patrick lit the Paschal fire, signifying the mystery of the Resurrection of Christ.
The choice of place was deliberate, since not many miles due south across the
river Boyne was the much lower hill of Tara, seat of the High Kings of Ireland,
where King Loígaire could not have failed to notice the fire lit in breach of his
decree.

MW

MICHAEL HEALY

Dublin 1873 - 1941 Dublin

31a A woman carrying a child

WATERCOLOUR OVER PENCIL ON PAPER 18.3 x 11.9 cms.

31b A donkey and cart

WATERCOLOUR OVER PENCIL ON PAPER 18.5 x 12.2 cms.

PROVENANCE Presented by Miss Evie Hone, 1953. N.G.I. 2560; 3260.

LITERATURE Le Harivel 1983, p. 246 (illus.).

Michael Healy was, besides being a stained glass artist of considerable merit, a consummate observer of life in his native city of Dublin. He was an extremely shy and reserved individual but, in his sketches, we appreciate him as a warm, sensitive and humane artist documenting the daily toil and travails of Dubliners. He worked long hours at the stained glass studio, **An Túr Gloine,** and his relaxation was to leave his lodgings at Pleasants Street, where he lived alone, and walk the streets sketching subjects quickly in his notebooks. He used a simple pencil and generally coloured in his drawings later with watercolours. But these images, like a *A woman carrying a child,* deceptively casual in appearance, are the keen-eyed testimony of an artist who loved his city and its people.

A donkey and cart is a good example of rapid pencil technique of Healy's. With half a dozen strokes of line he creates the well-massed form of a traveller seated on a donkey cart. The animal has an appealing, but weary, aspect causing us to appreciate the burden he is compelled to carry. The effect of Healy's drawings is that of an image we perceive with a quick glance. We do not recall details, just an impression of a fleeting moment. In this drawing we see a tiny isolated fragment of life in a city. The watercolour is added to the sketch, not with any special decorative intention but to give weight and body to the simple scene. Healy's sympathy is always with the poor. He spent some time as a postulant Dominican lay-brother at the novitiate in Tallaght but did not pursue this vocation. His drawings are, however, thoroughly imbued with a deep meditative spirit which favours those whose lot in life is not an easy one.

BPK

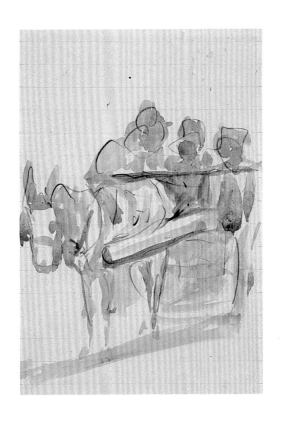

PAUL HENRY, R.H.A.

Belfast 1876 - 1958 Wicklow

*Paul Henry was the son of a Belfast Baptist Minister. He attended the Belfast School of Art before travelling to Paris to study at the Académie Julian and at Whistler's Académie Carmen. In 1900 he moved to London and began working as a book illustrator. He married a fellow artist, Grace Mitchell, in 1903. He first exhibited at the Royal Hibernian Academy in 1910 and, that same year, made a trip to Achill Island. He loved the place and decided to settle there in 1912. The scenery of the West of Ireland fascinated him and he began to paint landscapes which sought to capture the effects of the rapidly changing light which is so characteristic of the area. In 1919 he moved to Dublin and lived there until 1930 when he retired to County Wicklow. It was his great success as a landscapist, virtually creating an archetypal image of the West of Ireland, which finally sapped him of inspiration, but his best works are highly sensitive, intelligent and attractive images. When Grace died in 1951, he married Mabel Young. In his last years, he suffered from failing eyesight and from partial paralysis after a stroke. He wrote two volumes of autobiography, **An Irish Portrait** (1951) and **Further Reminiscences** (published posthumously in 1973).*

32 Isabella seeking Lorenzo's body in the forest, c.1906

CHARCOAL ON STRAWBOARD **40 x 33.2 cms.**

SIGNED **lower right,** *PAUL HENRY.*

INSCRIBED **on** *verso, No. 1.*

PROVENANCE **Bequeathed by Mrs Mabel F. Henry, the artist's widow, 1974. N.G.I. 7602.**

LITERATURE **Le Harivel, 1983, p. 277 (illus.).**

This drawing is tentatively dated to about 1906, the year in which Henry exhibited his work for the first time at a group show in the Goupil Gallery, London. He had been working in London as an illustrator for journals such as **Black and White, The Graphic** and **Today,** producing charcoal drawings of whatever subject he was prescribed by his editors. *Isabella seeking Lorenzo's body in the forest* is an illustration for the poem **'Isabella, or the Pot of Basil',** written by John Keats in 1820.

The story, from Boccaccio, tells how Isabella and Lorenzo fell in love, but to prevent their marriage he was murdered by her proud brothers. In a vision he describes to her his grave in the forest, amongst beeches and chestnuts. Isabella goes with her aged nurse to seek it and returns with Lorenzo's head which she conceals in a pot under sweet basil. In Henry's illustration the trees are bare of leaves and there are mushrooms growing on the ground. The nurse is clothed in a black cloak, carrying a stick in her left hand, and she stares vacantly in our direction from beneath the cowl of her long black cloak. Isabella, in contrast, is a young woman who wears a long white dress which she clutches above the knee with her right hand. From under her long hair, she looks out at us too. The drawing is confidently executed and serves to create a sombre mood, in keeping with the poem. The charcoal has been laid on in parallel strokes or with cross-hatching.

BPK

33 The Grand Canal Dock, Ringsend, Dublin, 1920s

CHARCOAL ON PAPER 40 x 33.2 cms.

SIGNED lower right, *PAUL HENRY*

INSCRIBED on backing paper, *THE GRAND CANAL DOCK, RINGSEND*

PROVENANCE Bequeathed by Mrs Mabel F. Henry, the artist's widow, 1974.
N.G.I. 7601.

LITERATURE Le Harivel, 1983, p. 277 (illus.); Kennedy, 1991, p. 20, plate 7.

The Grand Canal Dock, Ringsend, Dublin is untypical of Paul Henry's work in that it shows an industrial scene. Factory buildings in the Grand Canal Basin trail across the landscape and two tall chimneys rise up on the left each pumping dark smoke into the atmosphere. Small white puffs of smoke drift across the foreground. The buildings and chimneys are reflected in the water at the lower end of the drawing. The dock opened in the 1790s to link the Grand Canal with Dublin port. The two chimneys, known as 'The Tramway Twins', were constructed in 1900 by an American company for the Dublin United Tramway Company Ltd., as part of a power station on the south bank of the docks. They were demolished, with difficulty, in 1934 and 1943.

It is probable that the drawing dates to the 1920s when Henry was working in Dublin and had a studio at 13A Merrion Row. There is an oil painting derived from it (private collection). Henry was keenly involved in efforts to promote avant-garde painting and was a founder member of the Society of Dublin Painters. But his own style became fixed in the 1920s, and, even in this drawing, we see the emphasis on solid masses and the large areas of cloud and sky which became such a trademark in his landscapes of the West of Ireland. Henry's technique was soundly based and he was especially competent in the use of charcoal. In this drawing, we can discern how he has exploited the grain of the paper to good effect and, by rubbing heavily for dark tones and lightly for pale tones, has created a tightly finished urban landscape.

BPK

THOMAS HICKEY

Dublin 1741 - 1824 Madras

Thomas Hickey, the son of a Dublin
confectioner, received his early training at the
Dublin Society Schools before travelling to Italy
around 1761 to pursue his education. He
remained in Italy until 1767 when he returned
to Ireland, exhibiting ten portraits and one
subject picture at the Society of Artists in
Ireland over the period 1768-70. He then
moved to London where he entered the R.A.
schools in 1771. Between 1771-78 he exhibited
numerous works at the R.A., the last year
giving Bath as his address, having most likely
gone there, like many artists, to pursue a
clientele. Two years later he set sail for India,
but was captured en route and taken to Cadiz.
On his release he made his way to Lisbon
where he resumed his artistic activities and
painted a number of portraits, also subject
paintings. By 1784, Hickey had at last arrived
in India and was staying in Calcutta, where,
besides starting to paint again, he set about
writing a history of art, a project which did not
progress beyond the first volume. A short
return to England in 1791 was followed by a
further expedition to the Orient during the
years 1792-94, this time in the entourage of
Lord Macartney, who was travelling to Peking
and to whom he was attached as official
portrait painter. He may have revisited Dublin
in 1796, before again departing to the Orient,
this time accompanied by his daughters, in
1798. The final period of his career was spent
in India, passing time in Madras, Mysore, and
Calcutta, where his talents as a portraitist were
much in demand.

34 Portrait of Charles Lucas, 1758

CHARCOAL WITH WHITE HIGHLIGHTS ON GREY PAPER 46.5 x 36.5 cms.

SIGNED AND DATED lower right, T. Hickey 1758

PROVENANCE Purchased from P. Walsh and Son, Dublin, 1901. N.G.I. 2437.

LITERATURE Strickland 1913, vol. 1, p. 484. Dublin, London and Belfast 1969, p. 54;
Le Harivel 1983, p. 285 (illus.).

This attractive portrait of Charles Lucas, M.P., (1713-1771) is one of Hickey's
earliest essays in the art of portraiture. It is a remarkably accomplished work
for an artist of just seventeen, and already displays the considerable natural
talent and flair of the young Hickey for portraiture. Charles Lucas, the sitter,
had been born in 1713, probably at Ballingaddy, County Clare. After suffering a
reversal of fortunes, the family moved to Dublin where Lucas served his
apprenticeship as an apothecary, later setting up shop in Charles Street. Struck
by certain abuses relating to the sale of drugs, he published a pamphlet on the
problem in 1735, which resulted in the introduction of an Act for the inspection
of medicines. Chosen as one of the representatives of the Corporation in 1741,
he became critical of the manner in which the Board of Aldermen had usurped
many of the powers belonging by right to the entire Corporation, and along with
James La Touche, campaigned against such corruption.

Lucas became involved in national politics and promoted the idea of
parliamentary independence. Seeking election in 1749, it was determined that,
on the evidence of copies of his publications, he was an enemy of his country
and an order was issued for his arrest. He escaped to the Isle of Man and thence
to London where he stayed a short while before fleeing to Leyden in Holland,
where he graduated in medicine, in 1752. he then returned to England where he
remained for many years practising medicine and publishing on it. In 1761 he
obtained a pardon from the King and returned to Dublin where he was elected
M.P. for the city the same year. He continued to serve as a representative for
the city until his death. There is a later oil portrait of him by Hickey in the Royal
College of Physicians of Ireland. Edward Smyth carved a spirited full-length
marble figure (completed 1779), now in City Hall.

RK

EVIE HONE

Dublin 1894 · 1955 Dublin

*Evie Sydney Hone was born into a prosperous Dublin merchant family, a family which boasted several notable painters. Stricken by infantile paralysis at the age of eleven, the young lady nonetheless persevered in her ambition to become an artist. In London she studied with Byam Shaw, Walter Sickert and Bernard Meninsky; the last named advised her to study in Paris. With her close friend, Mainie Jellett, she went to Paris in 1920, studying first with André Lhote before moving to the studio of the strictly Cubist painter, Albert Gleizes. Each year for more than ten years she and Jellett went to learn from Gleizes, spending about three months on each visit. Evie Hone, a deeply spiritual person, was immensely moved by the work of Rouault, and by the glorious stained glass of Chartres Cathedral, which was but a short journey from Paris. Evie Hone's spiritual quest led her to join an Anglican convent at Truro, in Cornwall, for a short while in 1925; eventually, in 1937, she was received into the Church of Rome. Meanwhile, Rouault and Chartres Cathedral led her to do some small panels of stained glass, which she actually executed under the guidance of Wilhelmina Geddes at the latter's studio in London. Reluctantly she was accepted 'on approval' at **An Túr Gloine,** in 1933. The great discipline of her Cubist training, combined with her intuitive understanding of figurative painting, and of stained glass, led her to produce some of Western Europe's greatest stained glass in the first half of the twentieth century. The artist's friends recall that she regarded her windows for the chapel of the Jesuit Fathers at Tullabeg, County Offaly, and the three two-light windows in the east-facing apse of the Catholic Church at Kingscourt, County Cavan, as her best. These two series are imbued with a great feeling for Christianity and are also magnificent works of art, even though some critics might prefer the more hieratic glass of Michael Healy or Harry Clarke.*

35 The Crucifixion and The Last Supper, 1950

WATERCOLOUR AND GOUACHE WITH VARNISH ON PAPER 123 x 89 cms.

SIGNED AND DATED lower right, *Evie Hone 1950*

PROVENANCE Bequeathed by Mrs Nancy Connell, the artist's sister, St. Catherine's Park, Leixlip, County Kildare, 1958. N.G.I. 3302.

EXHIBITED I.E.L.A. 1952 (39c); Iserlohn 1955 (5); Dublin 1958 (45); London 1959 (66); London and New York 1967 (108).

LITERATURE Frost 1958, passim; White 1967, pp. 411-12; Le Harivel 1983, p. 288 (illus.); Bowe, Caron and Wynne 1988, p. 80, fig. 14.

This is the design for Evie Hone's best-known stained glass window, which replaced the great east window, shattered beyond repair during World War II, in Eton College Chapel. The Board of the College asked the late Earl of Crawford and Balcarres to find a suitable artist to design and execute a replacement for this jewel of English perpendicular Gothic. He agreed to do so. but only on condition that he could have two advisers, Kenneth Clark (later Lord Clark of Saltwood) and the Dean of York, an expert in mediaeval stained glass and theologically equipped to advise on iconographical matters. All English and worldwide practitioners could be considered, and there were many very competent persons, because of inter-war developments, and now the demand for the restoration of churches, or the construction of new ones. It was Sir Jasper Ridley who first drew Lord Crawford's attention to the work of Evie Hone. Lord Crawford came over to Evie Hone's studio, at Marlay, Rathfarnham, County Dublin. He then went to see some of her windows, particularly those at Tullabeg, County Offaly, and at Kingscourt, County Cavan. He invited her to submit a basic sketch design and convinced the College to accept it. Evie Hone's first proposal was to fill the entire window on the theme of the Resurrection, but the Dean of York objected to this on theological grounds. From this developed the scheme of the window as it is today: the lower register depicting the Last Supper (flanked by Melchizedek and the Sacrifice of Isaac), the upper the Crucifixion (below symbols of the Resurrection and Christ's miracles). Evie Hone worked assiduously at this enormous commission, and completed it between 1949 and 1952. It was a tremendous achievement, especially when one considers her physical disability, and her tenancity in executing several sections of the glass a number of times until she was happy that they were appropriate. For instance, the head of Christ, for the Crucifixion, did not blend in harmoniously with the neighbouring panels. This beautiful 'reject' was given to the late Lord Crawford, and she made another which she found to be suitable. If there is one criticism of Evie Hone's window, it has to be the fact that it is so powerful and rich that it draws all one's attention to such an extent that the visitor could easily leave the Chapel without noticing its splendid architectural acumen. This large watercolour shows the design fairly complete. An earlier study (N.G.I. 7856) and trial piece of glass with heads of two Apostles (N.G.I. 12,069) are also in the collection.

MW

Dublin *1894 - 1955* Dublin

36 The beach at Portrane, County Dublin, 1947

CHARCOAL AND GOUACHE ON PAPER 35 x 49 cms.

SIGNED AND DATED lower right, *E Hone. 1947.*

PROVENANCE Presented by Dr Françoise Henry, Dublin, 1977. N.G.I. 7796.

Taking breaks from a busy period of making stained glass, and even on holidays, Hone did not abandon her brushes. Invariably she worked in gouache, or sometimes in Indian ink, especially when sketching from medieval sculpture.

Portrane is on the north side of the estuary of the Broad Meadow Water and enjoys the sandy shores of north County Dublin. Situated at Portrane is a large hospital, St Ita's, visible in the distance. For all the freedom in the brushwork, she retains a cubist's artist's liking for interlocking shapes and flat colouring.

MW

NATHANIEL HONE THE YOUNGER, R.H.A.

Dublin 1831 · 1917 St Doulough's

*Nathaniel Hone was a member of the famous
artistic Hone family. He was the great grand-
nephew of Nathaniel Hone the Elder (1718-
1784) and a founder member of the Royal
Academy. Three of the latter's sons became
artists, and this artistic tradition has continued
into the twentieth century notably with Evie
Hone, the painter and stained glass artist. Hone
the Younger was the only painter in a
conventional family of merchants, bankers and
solicitors. He graduated with honours in
Engineering and Science from Trinity College,
Dublin, and began his career as an engineer
with the Midland Great Western Railway.
Suddenly at the age of twenty one he decided
to go to Paris to study art; his departure marks
a turning point in Irish art. Irish artists of earlier
generations had looked to England, or Rome,
for their training. Hone was the first Irish artist
of significance to go to Paris. His years there
corresponded with a vital time in French art
when the Realists and Barbizon artists were
beginning to challenge conventional Academic
Painting. When he moved to Barbizon Hone
remained there for almost thirteen years; he
became friendly with Corot, Millet and other
great landscape painters of the Barbizon
School. He was a contemporary of Monet,
Degas, Pissarro and Whistler and can be seen as
belonging to that important generation
between the Realists and the Impressionists.
Hone returned to Ireland at the age of forty,
married Magdalen Jameson of the wealthy
distilling family, and settled at Malahide,
vigorously pursuing his career as landscape
painter for the rest of his life. He can be
regarded as the first great Naturalistic painter
in Ireland. At first alone, but then followed by
Purser, Osborne, Kavanagh and others who had
also studied on the Continent, Hone introduced
French Naturalism into Irish Art.*

37 A line of windswept beeches

WATERCOLOUR OVER PENCIL ON PAPER 19.2 x 28.3 cms.

PROVENANCE Bequeathed by the artist's widow, Mrs Magdalen Hone, 1919. N.G.I.
6572.

LITERATURE O'Brien 1920, no. 821; Le Harivel 1983, p. 342 (illus.).

In Paris, Hone studied with Couture, who emphasised above all the practice of
making painted sketches. This is one of a number of sketches of trees in the
collection of the National Gallery and, although it is not possible to identify the
location, may have been painted shortly after Hone's return to Ireland in 1872.
He and Magdalen lived first at Seafield House, Malahide, later moving to
Moldowney House, just east of Malahide on the road to Portmarnock. Hone
continued to work on the type of subject matter that he had enjoyed painting in
France, like woodlands and pastures, and it can be difficult to distinguish
between the fields of Malahide and those of Barbizon. This is possibly a scene in
Malahide. Broad washes of paint define the distant hills and the gently rolling
green pasture land. The unfinished shapes in the right foreground were probably
intended to be sheep; on the *verso* of this sheet there is a study of **Sheep
beneath trees.** He uses several shades of green applied in layers to create a sense
of depth in the trees. Those in the foreground are more finished and defined.
They bend gently in the wind, and with quick, feather like brushstrokes the artist
has created a sense of the windswept branches. The fallen tree trunk in the left
foreground may tentatively be read as a motif remembered from the paintings of
the great seventeenth Dutch landscape painter Jacob van Ruisdael, whose work
we know Hone studied in the Louvre while still in Couture's studio.

FC

NATHANIEL HONE THE YOUNGER, R.H.A.

Dublin *1831 - 1917 St Doulough's*

38 The Propylaea, Athens, c.1892

WATERCOLOUR OVER PENCIL ON PAPER 11.8 x 19.5 cms.

EMBOSSED lower left, *NH*

PROVENANCE Bequeathed by the artist's widow, Mrs Magdalen Hone, 1919. N.G.I. 3425.

LITERATURE O'Brien 1920, no. 371; Le Harivel 1983, p. 312 (illus.).

Nathaniel Hone travelled widely, and at the age of sixty he set off on an extended tour of the Mediterranean reaching as far as Athens, Constantinople and Egypt. His journey is reflected in the many sketches he made along the way of some of the great monuments of antiquity. The Acropolis in Athens in particular inspired him as it has countless artists throughout the centuries, and numerous sketches exist of the Parthenon, the Agora, the Temple of Athena Nike and in this example, the Propylaea.

The word Propylon means a lobby or the entrance to a temple. It was in 437 BC that the architect Mnesikles designed the monumental entrances or Propylaea to lead up to the Parthenon. This was the largest and most beautiful building of its day; it was also extravagantly expensive, consisting of an entrance facade of Pentelic marble. The view Hone has chosen is of the north half of the central passage of the Propylaea, as seen from the west. The three columns in antis make a porch to the north wing of the Parthenon, on the left, and at right angles to the taller facade of the passage of the Propylaea. The room inside the wing formed the Picture Gallery, and is one of the earliest instances of a room specially built for this purpose. The foreground area, as in Hone's watercolour, is still today full of fallen stones and broken pieces of column.

FC

H. HULLEY

fl. London 1783 - 1790 Dublin

Very little indeed is known about this painter. He exhibited at the Royal Academy between 1783 and 1787, sending in his works from London addresses initially, and in 1787 from Bath. He came to Dublin, living first in Exchequer Street, and in 1790 in Abbey Street. After that year he has not been recorded. Strickland notes the sale of two pairs of works from two different collections in the nineteenth century; from his entry they would appear to have been oil paintings and all were landscapes.

39a Coastal scene with horse and cart

WATERCOLOUR ON PAPER 16.2 x 20 cms. (framed oval)

SIGNED lower right, *H. Hulley*

INSCRIBED in margin, lower right, *Capt. M*

39b Landscape with bridge, donkey and drover

WATERCOLOUR ON PAPER 16.8 x 19.8 cms. (framed oval)

INSCRIBED in margin, lower right, *Capt. M*

PROVENANCE Purchased, the pair, from James A. Gorry, Dublin, December 1981. N.G.I. 7950 and 7951.

EXHIBITED Dublin 1982 (37-38).

Given the paucity of information about Hulley, and the rarity of his works, it is difficult to assess his position art historically. The two watercolours exhibited here place him in the mainstream of late eighteenth century work, comparable to John Henry Campbell.

MW

MAINIE JELLETT

Dublin 1897 · 1944 Dublin

Mary Harriet 'Mainie' Jellett was a seminal figure in the history of twentieth century Irish art. She was born into a prosperous Dublin family; her father was a prominent barrister. All four daughters of the Jellett family acquired 'pet' names as children. 'Mainie' was educated privately and studied painting, initially with Elizabeth Yeats and Sarah Cecilia Harrison. She attended the Dublin Metropolitan School of Art before going to London to enrol under Walter Sickert at the Westminster Technical Institute. She won the Taylor Art Scholarship in 1920 and, the following year, she went to Paris, accompanied by Evie Hone, to study at André Lhote's Academy. She and Evie Hone then became students of Albert Gleizes, one of the original cubist group, and from 1922 they returned regularly to study with him for part of each year. Cubism was not a novelty in Paris but it was in Dublin. When Jellett exhibited two cubist paintings in Dublin in 1923, George Russell attacked them as 'artistic malaria'. Jellett travelled widely during the 1930s and was commissioned by the Irish Government to decorate the Irish Pavilion at the Glasgow Fair in 1937. She gained a reputation in Ireland as an excellent lecturer and broadcaster, promoting the modernist movement in art. In 1943 she was a founder member of the Irish Exhibition of Living Art. She was elected its first chairman but became ill before the first Irish Exhibition of Living Art show and died in Dublin in 1944, aged forty-six.

40 A water-lily pond, c.1919

GOUACHE ON PAPER 18 x 25 cms.

SIGNED lower right, M. Jellett

PROVENANCE Bequeathed by Miss R.S.R. Kirkpatrick, friend of the artist, 1979. N.G.I. 7849.

LITERATURE Le Harivel, 1983, p. 420 (illus.).

Mainie Jellett trained as a watercolourist with Elizabeth Yeats who gave weekly painting lessons at the Jellett household in Fitzwilliam Square. But when Jellett began to work as an abstract artist, an advocate of cubism, she relied less on watercolour and, instead, favoured the opaque medium of gouache. The density of this medium reinforced the cubist emphasis on the two-dimensional surface of a painting. *A water-lily pond* is an attractive image which exploits the decorative pattern-making of the water plants' leaves and flowers and probably dates from her first contact with cubism in London c.1919. The fluidity and movement is all on the surface. There is no explicit attempt to create depth. Jellett obeys her own dictum: 'The surface is my starting point, my aim is to make it live' (MacCarvill 1958, p. 50).

BPK

MAINIE JELLETT

Dublin 1897 - 1944 *Dublin*

41 Under the Big Top at a Circus

WATERCOLOUR WITH WHITE HIGHLIGHTS ON PAPER 40.5 x 49.5 cms.

PROVENANCE Purchased from The Neptune Gallery, Dublin, 1980. N.G.I. 18,153.

LITERATURE Le Harivel, 1983, p. 427 (illus.); Gillespie, Mooney and Ryan, 1986, p. 49 (illus.)

It is not possible to classify Mainie Jellett's output under one artistic style. She was Ireland's first and best cubist artist but she also produced excellent representational works like *Under the Big Top at a Circus.* She was meticulous in the creation of her pictures and the National Gallery of Ireland has two preparatory drawings for this watercolour. The first (N.G.I. 18,151) is a squared-up preliminary pencil drawing and the second is a more elaborate drawing (N.G.I. 18,152, wash on paper) which demonstrates the artists deletion of some elements and the development of others in order to achieve an organised surface layout. The final watercolour is full of interest, gaily coloured and carefully patterned. Two circus performers stand acrobatically on their prancing white horses while the ringmaster presides rigidly under the Big Top, cracking his whip. In the right foreground, two sad-faced clowns offer tragic-comic relief to the scene. Jellett's achievement is that she creates a picture which should be full of movement but its effect on us is that of a cinematic still photograph. The action is frozen in time and we concentrate on the geometric patterns and the flat colours.

BPK

THOMAS ALFRED JONES, P.R.H.A.

Dublin 1823 - 1893 Dublin

Jones was an orphan, adopted by the philanthropic Mr Archdale and his sisters. Showing an early interest in art, he was sent to the Royal Dublin Society Schools in 1833 and first exhibited (a scene from Macbeth) at the R.H.A. in 1841. In 1842 he began, but did not complete, a degree course at Trinity College, and from 1846-49 travelled abroad. Up to 1871 he exhibited a mixture of portraits, genre and subjects from Faust, in both watercolour and oil, but from 1872-93 oil portraits predominate. He was elected successively as an Associate and Member of the R.H.A. in 1860, then President in 1869. Well-liked in Dublin Society, he also made a large contribution towards building a new room for the R.H.A. Life School. Jones was knighted by the Lord Lieutenant in 1880, one of only four P.R.H.A. to have been so honoured.

42 Molly Macree, 1860s

WATERCOLOUR AND GOUACHE WITH GUM ARABIC ON PAPER 41 x 33.2 cms.

PROVENANCE Miss Beckett of Torquay, a friend of the artist; given by her to Miss M.A. Halligan, Torquay, by whom presented, 1947. N.G.I. 3025.

LITERATURE Le Harivel 1983, p. 447 (illus.); Gillespie, Mooney and Ryan 1986, p. 33 (illus.).

A glamorous young colleen with a bright shawl engages our attention as she looks directly at us. In an era following famine and mass emigration, such idealised images of Ireland were understandably popular and part of the received imagery of the countryside, with even William Thackeray sketching such a 'rustic beauty' for *The Irish Sketch Book* (1843, p. 225). There was a Victorian linking for similar pictures of rural life in Italy, a type that both Jones and Michael Brennan (1839-1871) painted in the 1860s, from when this watercolour probably dates. Jones exhibited related subjects of the *Colleen Bawn* (R.H.A. 1861), *The Colleen's Toilet* (R.H.A. 1864) and *A Limerick Lass* (Dublin 1865: 92), before he became an industrious, if dull, society portrait painter. There is a strong Pre-Raphaelite influence in both sentiment and technique, with small strokes of bright colour blended to give the feel of oil paint, though the work is thinly painted all over. The face is modelled by minute strokes of the same blue and red applied opaquely on the shawl to give a rich finish of jewel-like colour. The eye is drawn to the floral and neo-Celtic patterns on it, in contrast to the plain dress and stained apron below. The landscape is intentionally generalised, with the storm clouds that threaten rain on the cornfield and trees beyond, adding to the romantic mood of the piece.

ALH

HARRY KERNOFF, R.H.A.

London 1900 - 1974 Dublin

Aaron 'Harry' Kernoff was born in London, the son of a Russian-Jewish father and a Spanish mother. The family moved to Dublin in 1914 and his father established a business as a cabinet-maker. Harry Kernoff was apprenticed to his father's trade but attended evening classes at the Metropolitan School of Art and won the Taylor Art Scholarship in 1923. He lived in Dublin for the rest of his life, making few trips abroad, to the Soviet Union in 1930 and to Nova Scotia in the summer of 1958. He still travelled widely in Ireland and painted many of the colourful characters of Dún Chaoin and the Blasket Islands. He was much involved with the literary and theatrical figures of Dublin and painted most of them during his long career. He was elected as a member of the Royal Hibernian Academy in 1936 and exhibited at the annual exhibition every year until his death on Christmas Day, 1974.

43 Costumes for an officer, His daughter and a workman, 1928

WATERCOLOUR OVER INK AND PENCIL ON PAPER 17.8 x 22.5 cms.

SIGNED AND DATED lower right, *KERNOFF 28*

INSCRIBED *OFFICER IN RED. ACT 3 IN A MILITARY CAPE* (figure on left) *DAUGHTER ACT V IN BLACK* (centre figure) *WORKMAN IN WHITE BLOUSE.* (figure on right)

PROVENANCE Presented by Miss Lina Kernoff, the artist's sister, 1975. N.G.I. 3179.

LITERATURE Le Harivel, 1983, p. 465 (illus.).

Harry Kernoff was a noted 'character' in Dublin life, a member of the literary, artistic and theatrical scene which he recorded in a long career as a portraitist. He also worked as a book illustrator, theatre set and costume designer. His drawings such as *Costumes for an officer, his daughter and a workman* are delightful, witty and somewhat satirical in tone. They constitute what has been described as 'a visual dictionary of Irish types'. Kernoff portrayed people from all walks of life, sympathetically but accurately capturing their dress and mannerisms. Pomposity and pseudo-sophistication are the special targets of his keen artistic eye. The National Gallery of Ireland has a large collection of Kernoff's portrait drawings and costume designs. Some of the latter were prepared for productions at the Gate Theatre which was founded by Micheál MacLiammoir and Hilton Edwards in 1928, the year in which this particular drawing was executed. Kernoff visited the Soviet Union in the 1920s and was much influenced by Russian designers. This gave his drawings a cosmopolitan air which allowed him to reveal the bohemian society which existed in Dublin during the sober years of the Irish Free State (1922-48). The paradox of these decades was that artistic temperaments were stirred to give their talents full expression, aroused by the blatant hostility of the censorship laws. Curiously, however, the theatre was never offically censored in Ireland unlike the cinema and book publishing. Perhaps this was because the theatre-going public tended to deliver its verdict in demonstrative fashion as in the case of the riotous disturbances provoked by the production of Seán O' Casey's *The Plough and the Stars* at the Abbey Theatre in 1926.

BPK

OFFICER. IN RED

ACT 3.
IN A
MILITARY
CAPE

DAUGHTER.
ACT V
IN BLACK

441

WORKMAN IN
WHITE BLOUSE

KERNOFF 28

44 The Boer War Memorial, St Stephen's Green, Dublin, 1935

PENCIL ON CARD 23.2 x 27.6 cms.

INSCRIBED lower left corner, *Stephen's Gn. N.W. During a tram strike Dublin May 14, '35*

PROVENANCE Presented by Miss Lina Kernoff, the artist's sister, 1975. N.G.I. 3194.

EHXIBITED Dublin 1988 (-).

LITERATURE Le Harivel, 1983, p. 467 (illus.).

Although Harry Kernoff was born in London, not Dublin, he became a quintessential artist of Ireland's capital city, recording its citizens and its architectural and cultural heritage. The Boer War Memorial (known colloquially as "Traitor's Gate") which stands on the corner of St Stephen's Green, opposite Grafton Street, was erected as a memorial to soldiers of the Royal Dublin Fusiliers who were killed in the Boer War (1899-1902). This was a particularly brutal war marked by guerrilla raids, scorched earth policies and the 'concentration camps' or internment centres established in 1900 by Kitchener, the British Commander-in-Chief, in an attempt to isolate Boer resistence groups. Kitchener was born near Ballylongford, County Kerry, and many other famous Irishmen fought in the war including Erskine Childers and James Craig (Lord Craigavon) for the British forces, and John MacBride who led an Irish brigade which fought on the Boer side.

Kernoff's lightly drawn sketch of the Memorial Arch reminds us of by-gone days when traffic flowed in both directions around the Green and the pace of life was more leisurely. But the recent stone cleaning of the Memorial by the Office of Public Works and the growth in the number of jarveys offering horse-drawn carriage trips around St Stephen's Green and its environs are welcome developments. This drawing was a preparatory sketch for a painting **The North-West Corner of St Stephen's Green** (private collection) which was exhibited at the R.H.A. in 1936 (66) and sold at James Adam & Sons in 1984 (24 May, lot 37).

BPK

WILLIAM JOHN LEECH, R.H.A.

Dublin 1881 - 1968 Guildford

The son of the Regius Professor of Law at Trinity College, Dublin, William Leech was educated at St Columba's College, Rathfarnham, and at the Metropolitan School of Art, before enrolling at the Royal Hibernian Academy School under Walter Osborne. In 1901 he went to Paris to study with Bouguereau and Laurens at the Atelier Julian and, two years later, went to Brittany, settling at Concarneau. He won the Taylor Art Scholarship in 1905 and again in 1906. He was elected as a Member of the Royal Hibernian Academy in 1910. He lived in Brittany from 1903 to 1910 when he moved to London, later settling in the South of England.
He continued to exhibit with the Royal Hibernian Academy, the New English Art Club and the Royal Academy. He was represented at the important exhibitions of Irish Art at Paris in 1922 and at Brussels in 1930. He married May Botterell in 1953 and died at Guildford, Surrey in 1968.

45 A snow-covered field, c.1910

WATERCOLOUR OVER CHARCOAL ON PAPER 51.7 x 35.8 cms.

SIGNED lower right, Leech -

PROVENANCE Purchased from Mr Alan Denson (on behalf of the artist's niece), 1968. N.G.I. 6878.

EXHIBITED Dallas 1976 (72).

LITERATURE Le Harivel, 1983, p. 472 (illus.).

The work of William Leech is beginning only now, over twenty years after his death, to receive the serious attention it merits. In quality, subject range and technique, he was an outstanding artist. He travelled widely in Europe before settling in England in 1916. He continued to exhibit in Paris and Dublin contributing to the Royal Hibernian Academy annual exhibition nearly every year until his death in 1968.

Leech's watercolours are atmospheric and impressionistic. *A snow-covered field* is a sensitive drawing of two saplings in the foreground, at the base of a snow-covered hill. A wooden fence divides the scene and there is a clump of bare trees above it to the left. The artist demonstrates the effects of nature in an impressionistic manner which makes the viewer appreciate the airy expanse of the scene and the cold snowy climate. The drawing was probably painted in Switzerland in 1910 or 1911. Alan Denson recalls in a letter (NGI archive) that Leech told him that he had painted some snow scenes there at that time. Leech retained a love of landscape throughout his career and even while he was busy working on portraits, he painted many landscapes in watercolour for his own pleasure.

BPK

WILLIAM JOHN LEECH, R.H.A.

Dublin 1881 · 1968 Guildford

46 A mountain view, c.1910

WATERCOLOUR OVER CHARCOAL ON PAPER 49.8 x 34.8 cms.

SIGNED lower left, *Leech -*

PROVENANCE Purchased from Mr Alan Denson (on behalf of the artist's niece), 1968. N.G.I. 6879.

EXHIBITED Dallas 1976 (73); Dublin and Belfast 1984-85 (120).

LITERATURE Le Harivel, 1983, p. 472 (illus.).

This mountain scene has been variously described as 'A Mountain View' and 'A Mountain Town or Monastery'. Like *A snow-covered field,* it was probably painted in Switzerland in 1910 or 1911. A green hill in the foreground is surmounted by a mountain beyond it, painted in a warm cobalt, on the peak of which a complex of buildings, probably a monastery, is situated. The sky is green, touched with a rust colour.

In this work, we see a good example of Leech's interest in perspectives from unusual angles. The town or monastery is drawn from below so that we are given the impression of a steep mountainous incline, many hundreds of metres in height. The strange shapes of the mountains and the almost graphic effect of the patterns etched by the cliff edges are characteristic features of many of Leech's watercolours. Thomas Bodkin's comment in 1909 about a Leech painting is equally appropriate to this watercolour: 'charming for its atmospheric clearness, good perspective and other artistic points, which almost make the spectator think he is looking at a real scene instead of a picture' (Bodkin 1909, p. 5).

BPK

Maurice MacGonigal's father was a Sligo-born master painter and decorator. He was educated by the Christian Brothers, Synge Street, Dublin, and, aged fifteen, entered the stained glass studio of his uncle, Joshua Clarke. He was actively involved in the struggle for Irish Independence and was arrested and interned in 1920. After the Treaty in 1922, he rejected active politics and returned to stained glass work. In 1923 he won a scholarship to the Metropolitan School of Art and the Taylor Art Scholarship. His teachers were Seán Keating, James Sleator and Patrick Tuohy. He gradually abandoned stained glass and took up painting full-time. He first exhibited at the Royal Hibernian Academy in 1924 and exhibited annually there for the next fifty-four years. He was elected an Academician in 1933 and, that same year, became Keeper of the R.H.A. He began teaching at the R.H.A. School and at the Metropolitan School of Art where in 1930, he was appointed Assistant Professor of Painting. He became Professor of Painting at the R.H.A. in 1947 and President of the Academy in 1962, in succession to Keating. He designed posters, stage sets, and worked as a book illustrator besides producing many oil paintings and watercolours. He died in 1979 and was buried at Roundstone, County Galway.

47 The Dropping Well Public House, Dartry, 1922/23

WATERCOLOUR AND GOUACHE ON PAPER 53 x 48 cms.

SIGNED lower right, *MAURICE McGONIGAL*

INSCRIBED ON REVERSE *From view at Milltown Maurice MacGonigal Metropolitan School of Art Kildare Str Dublin Ireland Homes and Gardens Competition.*

PROVENANCE Purchased from the artist by Miss Cunningham and presented by her to Charlotte Lane McGuinness on the occasion of her marriage to H.E. St G. MacClenaghan, 14 September 1927; thence by descent to Mrs MacClenaghan's son, K.P. MacClenaghan, from whom purchased, 1982. N.G.I. 18,487.

EXHIBITED Dublin 1982 (39).

LITERATURE Le Harivel, 1983, p. 486 (illus.); Gillespie, Mooney and Ryan 1986, p. 48 (illus.); Dublin 1991, pp. 10-11 (illus.).

The Dropping Well Public House, Dartry, depicts a popular licensed premises situated close to the river Dodder. Maurice MacGonigal's attractive watercolour dates from the early 1920s and shows The Dropping Well to the left of the Old Bridge at Dartry (Classon's Bridge) which has since been rebuilt. The Dodder and its many bridges had been a favourite subject of Dublin painters for centuries and MacGonigal exploits the area's scenic potential in an appealing manner. The drawing is well-structured as one would expect from an artist undergoing strict academic training at the Metropolitan School of Art. There is a freshness of approach in the way the artist lays on his washes with particular emphasis on the play of light and shadows. There are some traces of MacGonigal's background as a stained glass artist in the rather stylised use of line and the massing of colours. Few such watercolours by him survive, as MacGonigal himself destroyed a large number.

BPK

DANIEL MACLISE, R.H.A., R.A.

Cork 1806 - 1870 London

Son of a Cork shoemaker, Maclise received a sound elementary education which gave him a life-long interest in books and classical literature. Though he first found employment in banking, he was able from 1822 to pursue an artistic education at the newly established School of Art. More good fortune followed in the person of Sir Walter Scott, who, when he visited Cork in 1825, admired the portrait the young artist had sketched of him, and encouraged him in his career. Richard Sainthill, the distinguished antiquarian, became his patron and advised him to go to London to complete his training, advice Maclise followed in 1827. He initially earned his keep with portraits and illustrations for various publications, including **Fraser's Magazine,** *to which he submitted a portrait of his lifelong friend, Charles Dickens, but Maclise soon developed a substantial reputation as a subject painter, a branch of painting which suited his bookish nature. Although he visited Paris on a number of occasions and knew French art, the most important influence on his work was that of the German Nazarenes. His approach to subject painting was characterised by a keen sense of history and theatricality, showing attention to detail, on which he evidently did considerable research. While his earlier compositions exhibit a somewhat sentimental approach, later creations are more ambitious and achieve a sense of grandeur. From 1846, he received a series of major commissions for the Palace of Westminster, which culminated in his frescoes depicting* **The meeting of Wellington and Blücher** *(1861) and* **The Death of Nelson** *(1865).*

48 The Marriage of Strongbow and Aoife, c.1854

WATERCOLOUR ON PAPER 51.2 x 80.2 cms.

SIGNED lower left, D. MACLISE - RA. PINXT

PROVENANCE J. Boughton Dugdale; Sir Victor Caillard; Dr Roger Wright; Christie's, 14 November 1967, lot 136, bought by Agnew's, London, from whom purchased, 1967. N.G.I. 6315.

EXHIBITED Manchester 1887 (1653); London 1896 (133); London and Dublin 1972 (105).

LITERATURE Ormond 1968, p. 693; Turpin 1970, pp. 190-92; Le Harivel 1983, p. 493 (illus.); Gillespie, Mooney and Ryan 1986, p. 25 (illus.); Butler 1990, pp. 126 (illus.), 158-59, fig. 172.

The watercolour represents the marriage of Princess Aoife, daughter of Dermot McMorrough, King of Leinster, and the Norman, Richard de Clare, known as Strongbow. This event occurred after the Battle of Waterford in 1170 and marked the consolidation of the Norman foothold in Ireland, giving their presence a legitimacy, whch heralded the ruin of the native Irish Princes. It is this aspect of the union which Maclise represents, the marriage being enacted against a ruined church, with the city of Waterford burning in the background. The marriage is seen not only as a politically significant union, but also a socially and culturally destructive event, with the native way of life, as symbolised by its defeated army, its womenfolk, the toppled Celtic cross and silent bard, gone forever. The bristling armoury of the powerfully equipped Norman soldiers dominates the centre of the composition and makes a startling contrast to the dead and subjugated native forces in the foreground. The whole episode is given a solemn and tragic air, but treated in a heroic manner, reminiscent of the great masters of the Renaissance, and their more contemporary German followers, the Nazarenes. Maclise's love of history and talent for storytelling, as well as his taste for well researched archaeological detail, are superbly evident in this monumental composition, which received its definitive treatment in the great canvas also in the collection (N.G.I. 205). This gigantic work, which differs in a number of details from the present watercolour, was originally commissioned for the Palace of Westminster, where the Fine Arts Commissioners wished it to be painted in fresco. The watercolour is dated close to 1854, when the oil was exhibited at the Royal Academy.

RK

JAMES MAHONY, A.R.H.A.

Cork 1810 · 1879 London

*Son of a carpenter, Mahony is said to have studied in Rome before returning to Cork in 1842, to establish himself as a watercolour painter. He exhibited French and Italian views at the R.H.A. from 1842-46, also literary subjects. Mahony again travelled abroad, particularly in Spain. He was elected an Associate of the R.H.A. in 1856, when he showed 17 watercolour views and historical subjects, including a number from the 1855 Taylor Bequest to the N.G.I. His large panoramic views of Dublin and Spain date from this time. In 1859 he moved permanently to Marylebone in London, beginning a second career as illustrator, while exhibiting at the Royal Academy 1866-77 and becoming an Associate of the New Watercolour Society in 1867. He worked for the **Illustrated London News** on current events, such as the famine in Skibbereen, and illustrated serials for **Sunday at Home** (1865-66) and **Leisure Hour** (1867). His work is also found in **Sunday Magazine** (1866-71), Cassell's Magazine (1867), **Good Works for the Young** (1869), **London Magazine** (1870) and other publications. In the 'Household edition' of Dickens, he illustrated **Oliver Twist, Little Dorrit** and **Our Mutual Friend.***

49 Aerial view of Dublin from the spire of St George's, Hardwicke Place, 1854

WATERCOLOUR OVER INK ON PAPER 105 x 164.7 cms.

SIGNED AND DATED lower left, on a garden wall, *JAMES MAHONY. 1854*

PROVENANCE Bequeathed by Captain George Archibald Taylor, 1855. N.G.I. 2450.

EXHIBITED R.H.A. 1856 (187); Dublin 1988 (-).

LITERATURE Le Harivel 1983, p. 494 (illus.); de Courcy and Maher 1985, p. 18 (illus.).

This tour de force shows the expanse of Victorian Dublin from the north side of the city, viewed out of the spire of Francis Johnston's neo-classical St George's Church (1802-13) on Hardwicke Place. A small ink and wash study (Civic Museum) was done there, with this watercolour, the largest in the National Gallery of Ireland, worked up in his studio. In the foreground he surveys (from the left) Mountjoy Square, the last Georgian square, with figures promenading in the gardens; Gardiner's place and its busy intersection at Hill Street, with Old St George's tower; Great Denmark Street and the rear of Belvedere House; tradesmen and passersby on North Great George's Street; the stables flanking tiny Rutland Street West and the corner of Rutland (now Parnell) Square, with the Rotunda Hospital and gardens below the sedan chair shelter (now gone). In a central band, main features are highlighted in gouache, with rooflines delineated without ink so as to avoid the hard edge of 18th century topography. We see Dublin Bay and the flat land not yet built over with docks; George's dock, with ships right up behind Amiens Street (now Connolly) Station; Gandon's Custom House; the Pro-Cathedral (Sweetman and Papworth), parallel to the General Post Office on Sackville (now O'Connell) Street (*see detail*), where Mahony includes minute omnibuses, carters and a troup of cavalry. Across the river Liffey, packed with shipping, the railway disappears left towards Kingstown (now Dun Laoghaire); the Irish Industrial Exhibition building stands on Leinster Lawn; Van Nost the Younger's George II is still on St Stephen's Green; the full expanse of Trinity College (in sunlight) is seen against the blue outline of County Wicklow and the Great Sugar Loaf Mountain, while the former Parliament House does not stand out. The panorama ends with City Hall and Dublin Castle. Mahony may have been inspired to rival the large woodcut aerial view of Dublin published by the *Illustrated London News* in 1846 (N.G.I. 11,878), but taken from the other side of the city. Urban panoramas from a camera obscura were popular at the time, that of 1853 in Edinburgh is still in use. Captain G.A. Taylor bequeathed eighty 19th century watercolours to the collection and may have commissioned this work.

ALH

(detail).

JAMES MAHONY, A.R.H.A.

Cork *1810 · 1879* London

50 The Visit by Queen Victoria and Prince Albert to the Fine Art Hall of The Irish Industrial Exhibition, Dublin, c.1853

WATERCOLOUR ON PAPER 62.8 x 81 cms.

PROVENANCE purchased from The Fine Art Society, London, 1969. N.G.I. 7009.

LITERATURE Crookshank and Glin 1978, p. 195, fig. 187; Crookshank 1979, p. 38 (illus.); Le Harivel 1983, p. 497 (illus.).

Queen Victoria and Prince Albert visited the Irish Industrial Exhibition on four mornings from August 30 to September 2, 1853. It was in a temporary building on Leinster Lawn, a third, the size of the 1851 London Great Exhibition building of steel and glass. Its Sligo-born architect, Sir John Benson, used wood, glass and some iron, as he had for the 1852 Cork Exhibition. Mahony recorded the State Reception (N.G.I. 2453), the last visit (N.G.I. 2452) and here the second, with some invention, when more than an hour was spent in the Picture Gallery (*The Times* 2.9.1853, p. 6). The Royal couple are at the centre with Princes Alfred and Arthur to the right in kilts. He left no key to the R.H.A. Members and welcoming party in the detailed foreground band. This main Fine Art Hall, housing contemporary art, was 325 feet long, 40 feet broad and 38 feet high, with the central Great Hall to the right of this view, Old Masters and Irish Antiquities in a smaller room to the left, and the Medieval Hall beyond, leading into Leinster House. Giant wooden (unpainted) beams supported the roof, with greyish-green frosted glass in the central skylight only, to control the flow of light. Prince Albert congratulated Benson on solving the problem of lighting a Picture Gallery. One wall was lined with British and Irish paintings, the other with Continental ones. Mahony indicates portraits above subject pieces, on a pink material, but they are not painted in detail. Royal portraits by Winterhalter, *Daniel O'Connell* (Wilkie), *The Deluge* (Danby) and *Joan of Arc charging in a sortie* (Etty) should be visible. Several pieces of sculpture are imagined but *Hibernia with a bust of Lord Cloncurry* (Hogan), *Eve* (MacDowell) and *Boys wrestling* (Lalor) are on the left, with the reclining *Drunken faun* (Foley) and *Youth at the stream* (Foley) on the right, though the latter is not in the catalogue. Nor were gothick thrones put out on this visit. The coat of arms in the border includes the three castle Dublin city emblem, while a relief medallion of William Dargan (who underwrote the heavy losses of the exhibition and specified a separate section for the fine arts), is garlanded with shamrock and inscribed *An uair is dorcha sé an uair roimh breacadh an lae* (the darkest hour is the hour before the dawn) an allusion no doubt to Ireland's expected cultural and political resurgence.

ALH

JAMES MALTON

London c.1760 - 1803 London

Malton was one of three members of a family
associated with recording architecture. His
father Thomas Malton the Elder (1726-1801)
wrote and lectured on geometry and
perspective and lived in Dublin from the 1780s.
His brother, Thomas Malton the Younger (1748-
1804) painted and engraved views of Bath and
London. James Malton is thought to have
worked in James Gandon's office but later
turned against him. Malton's reputation rests
on his twenty-five views of Dublin, engraved in
aquatint, and issued individually from 1792-99,
when they appeared bound with a commentary
as **A Picturesque and descriptive view of the city
of Dublin,** stating in the preface that 'the entire
of the views were taken in 1791, by the
Author'. 'Malton's Dublin has been called one
of the most beautiful books of the art of
aquatint. Though it is only the third illustrated
book on Dublin ever to appear, its predecessors
being Walter Harris's **History** of 1766 and Poole
and Cash's **Views** of 1780, it is unlikely that
anything comparable will ever be done again'
(Craig 1984, p. vii). Prior to the production of
the aquatints, it would appear that Malton
executed large size watercolours, though these
are not followed precisely. The biggest group of
these is now in the National Gallery of Ireland;
others are found in Trinity College, Dublin (1);
the Victoria and Albert Museum, London (2);
Mount Stewart House, County Down (1) and
the Huntington Library, at San Marino,
California (2).

51 The Custom House, Dublin, 1793

WATERCOLOUR OVER INK ON PAPER 53.6 x 77 cms.

SIGNED AND DATED lower left, James Malton del. 1793.

PROVENANCE Purchased at Christie's, 25 May, 1914, lot 97. N.G.I. 2705.

ENGRAVED Related to the artist's own aquatint, published by him in London and G.
Cowen in Dublin, July 1792 (N.G.I. 11,640).

EXHIBITED R.A. 1793 (838); Dublin 1975 (141); Bordeaux 1977 (37); Dublin 1988 (-).

LITERATURE Le Harivel 1983, p. 498 (illus.); Craig 1984, no. 9; McParland 1985, pp.
46ff., plate 41; de Courcy and Maher 1985, p. 15 (illus.); Butler 1990, p. 37,
fig. 33.

The Custom House (1781-91) is arguably the finest public building in Dublin and
built to the design of James Gandon; his other important works are the Four
Courts (1786-96) and the King's Inns (1795-1816), while in County Laois he
created a magnificient neo-classical country house, Emo Court, County Leix
(1791-98), for the Earls of Portarlington. The construction of the Custom House
was on a superb site along the river Liffey, at a point used heavily by ships. The
view from upstream was later wrecked by the railway bridge alongside Butt
Bridge. Other views remain intact. The building was gutted by fire in 1921, and
the interior apartments of John Beresford, Commissioner of Revenue, were lost.
The dome was rebuilt with Ardbraccan limestone, rather than Portland stone,
which has now darkened.

The building is graced by much sculpture; swags, trophies and the famous key-
stones of Irish river gods being an integral part of the architectural design. A
figure of Commerce crowns the dome, Neptune, Mercury and allegorical figures
are over the pediment, with its representation of Hibernia embracing Brittania.
The team of sculptors was led by Edward Smyth, who frequently collaborated
with Gandon. In recent years considerable sums were spent on cleaning,
reinforcing and improving the appearance of this gracious building. The weather,
and pollution, had taken their toll, particularly on the sculptures. The date on
the watercolour (1793) is later than that of the related aquatint (July 1792). It is
not the only case of this phenomenon and it is possible that those watercolours
bearing dates after the publication of the aquatints, were signed and dated by
Malton in order to confirm his authorship of them. Figure variations occur
between watercolour and print, which is just what one would expect from a
draughtsman who is his own engraver. A trial etching, with added watercolour,
is in the collection (N.G.I. 11,634).

MW

52 The Tholsel, Dublin, 1792

WATERCOLOUR OVER INK ON PAPER 42.4 x 58.8 cms.

SIGNED AND DATED lower left, *James Malton del 1792*

ENGRAVED in aquatint by the artist, published by him in London and G. Cowen in Dublin, June 1793 (N.G.I. 11,574).

PROVENANCE Presented by William M. Smith, 1872. N.G.I. 2185.

EXHIBITED R.A. 1793 (843); Dublin 1975 (136).

LITERATURE Strickland 1913, vol. 2, p. 97; Craig 1952, pp. 47-48; Rothery 1978, p. 22 (illus.); Le Harivel 1983, p. 477 (illus.); Craig 1984, no. 11.

The Tholsel, seen in this watercolour by James Malton, was pulled down in 1806 because it was in poor repair. It was constructed in 1676 by the Master-builder Thomas Graves, who may well have designed it also, inspired by similar buildings in Great Britain and Ireland. The ground floor was an arcade; above was a suite of rooms such as the Council Room, the Court Room, and some offices. A drawing by Thomas Dineley, of 1680, shows some superstructures, which, most likely, were made with timber, and which had been removed well before Malton executed his watercolour.

The Tholsel was used for the type of business conducted in the City Hall today; the arms of the City of Dublin can be seen in the centre of the balcony parapet immediately over the main doorway to the building. Given the very few seventeenth century buildings remaining in Dublin today, it is a pity that the Tholsel did not survive. It stood in Skinners' Row, close to Christ Church Cathedral.

MW

WILLIAM MULREADY, R.A.

Ennis 1786 - 1863 London

Though born in Ennis, County Clare, Mulready moved to London at a very early age and received all his artistic education there. He first studied in the studio of sculptor Thomas Banks where he spent a year (1799) learning to draw, and copying from antique casts. In 1800, he gained admission to the Royal Academy Schools studying under Johann Heinrich Füseli and by the time he was eighteen he was exhibiting at the annual R.A. exhibitions. Early in his career he earned an income by assisting John Varley with drawing classes and by illustrating children's books. Varley encouraged him to go on sketching trips, a practice he took to readily, and he quickly developed a keen eye with landscape, for which he had a definite talent. He soon abandoned landscape in favour of genre painting, a decision possibly influenced by his friendship from 1808 with David Wilkie. The demand for small scenes illustrating domestic scenes was very strong and Mulready found a ready market for his keenly observed and beautifully crafted compositions which were normally marked by their sentimental nature, frequently tinged with moralising theme. He had a particular gift for illustrating subjects with children. His achievements won him much recognition, most notably the Legion of Honour for excellence in 1855, when he exhibited at the Exposition Universelle. He was elected an A.R.A. in 1815 and became a full R.A. the next year. His finely detailed, richly coloured compositions, were an influence on the art of the Pre-Raphaelites.

53 Study for 'The Sonnet', c.1839

PENCIL AND RED CHALK, WITH WHITE HIGHLIGHTS ON PAPER 36 x 29.9 cms.

SIGNED lower right, WM... *(indecipherable date)*

LITHOGRAPHED by John Linnell Junior, 1848 (repr. Stephens 1890).

PROVENANCE Purchased at T. Horrocks Millar sale, Christie's 14 July 1933, lot 21. N.G.I. 2950.

EXHIBITED R.A. 1845 (955); R.A. 1848 (70); R.A. 1864 (207); Dallas 1976 (24); North Carolina etc. 1983 (pp. 162-63); London, Dublin and Belfast 1986-87 (161).

LITERATURE Wilson 1964; Heleniak 1980, p. 214, no. 151; Le Harivel 1983, p. 561 (illus.); Butler 1990, pp. 142, 144.

Mulready was a consummate draughtsman and his graphic work was much admired during his lifetime. Joseph Farrington remarked in his diary (16 November, 1807) 'Mulready a young man twenty one or two of age is reckoned to draw the best, but gets Himself high upon it as if He had done His business'. Mulready continued the practice of drawing from the life throughout his career. The present work is a finished study of the composition he painted in 1839 for his most important patron, John Sheepshanks. The subject, a young couple who are almost certainly romantically involved, was typical of the artist, who drew on everyday life as the source of inspiration for his art. In an idyllic rural setting, a girl reads the sonnet she has received from a bashful young man. It was Mulready's belief that genre painting could rise to the level of high art through the dedication and skill of the artist. An important aspect of this philosophy of art was the great attention given to drawing and the preparation of carefully worked up studies followed by highly finished canvases. Mulready wrote in his Account Book 'Jan 15. Feb. 8.10 Cartoon of Sonnet'. The design differs in only one detail from the finished painting, the small clump of trees to the upper left of the composition do not appear in the final, painted version. When exhibited in 1839, the painting drew the following comment from the *Art Union* (No. 5, 1839, p. 81) '...were it permitted to talk of living British artists, I might tell of a little picture called *The Sonnet* of a spans breadth, which reminds the spectator of the magnificent genius of MichaelAngelo in the Sistine Chapel'. It is now in the Victoria and Albert Museum, London.

RK

HENRY NEWTON

fl. Dublin 1840 - 1856 *Dublin*

*Little is known of Henry Newton except that he
was an English artist who settled in Dublin and
lived for some time at Booterstown. From 1847
he exhibited at the Royal Hibernian Academy,
contributing at intervals until 1856.*

54 Below Esna Larach Waterfall, Glenarrif, County Antrim

WATERCOLOUR WITH GUM ARABIC ON PAPER 90.5 x 69.8 cms.

PROVENANCE Bequeathed by Captain George Archibald Taylor, 1855. N.G.I. 2481.

LITERATURE Strickland 1913, vol. 2, p. 170; Le Harivel 1983, p. 569 (illus.).

Watercolours were regarded as drawings by the Royal Academicians and
subsequently had always been given an inferior place in the Academy's
exhibitions. Indeed, watercolour artists were regarded as amateurs. The
example of watercolourists on the Continent, such as Hackert and Ducros,
encouraged their English counterparts in the campaign to establish their art on a
higher academic plane. At the turn of the century Turner transformed
topographical views by his use of herioc and dramatic effects of light and
atmosphere, sparking a controversy which lasted throughout the first half of the
nineteenth century as to the relative merits of the two media. Newton, about
whom so little is known, came from this background, and his work embodies
some of the predominant principles of teaching in watercolours in the early
nineteenth century. Several nineteenth century treatises discussed the
phenomenon of light, colour and vision, urging the use of scientific accuracy, yet
not to the exclusion of the ideal. Newton produced sublime or 'beautiful'
subjects perceived with an observant eye; he must have been aware of the
teaching of John Varley, a drawing master associated with the Water-Colour
Society. In Varley's *A Treatise on the Principles of Landscape* of 1815, he shows
his reader how to analyse and arrange pictorial effects according to principles of
contrast, balance and eye movements.

Glenarrif is one of the more beautiful of the nine glens of Antrim; the finest part
of the Glen is notable for its waterfalls and Esna Larach is the largest of these.
Newton has created a 'picturesque' view; he has painted the scene from below
the waterfall thus enabling him to include a foreground area of calmer water.
Great curtains of foliage flank the waterfall, and a shaft of light cuts a diagonal
through its zig-zag path thus creating a sense of balance in the centre of the
composition. The dramatic effect of the surging waterfall slicing through the
rock is enhanced by the contrast with the stillness of the boulders and the small
white crane. His concern is with the structure and surface texture of the
rockface and the tonal changes in the expanses of foliage, yet in the foreground
the rocks are more broadly handled and the water in places consists of little
more than a weak biscuit-coloured wash that barely covers the paper surface.
Newton exhibited views of Esna Larach at the R.H.A. in 1850 (188) and 1856
(327). There is a smaller version in the collection (N.G.I. 2204).

RK

ANDREW NICHOLL, R.H.A.

Belfast 1804 - 1886 London

*Son of a Belfast boot and shoe maker, Nicholl received no formal education as an artist, first embarking on a career as a compositor for F.D. Finlay c.1824, working on the **The Northern Whig**. This newspaper first proclaimed the aspiring artist's promise. Having made a series of views of the Antrim coast in 1828, he travelled to London in 1830, where he spent time copying the Old Masters at the Dulwich Picture Gallery. Moving back to Belfast, he had his first small exhibition in the Commercial Buildings and took up teaching art to supplement his income. He was already specialising in landscape art, more specifically topographical views. For the next sixteen years he travelled frequently between Belfast and London, also in Ireland, painting views of the most notable beauty spots, sometimes for publications. In 1830, the Duchess of Northumberland acquired eight views by Nicholl for her collection. His first important commission was from W.A. Ackermann in 1832 for a set of views of the Western Highlands. In the same year he started to contribute to the newly established **Dublin Penny Journal**. In 1846 he left for Ceylon where he took the post of Master of drawing and painting at the Columbo Academy. On his return from Ceylon (probably in 1849), Nicholl first settled in Belfast, before establishing himself more permanently in London, though he continued to visit Dublin. He was elected an A.R.H.A. in 1837 and full Academician in 1860.*

55 Belfast and Cave Hill from Newtownbreda Church

WATERCOLOUR ON PAPER 52 x 87.3 cms.

SIGNED lower right, *A. Nicholl R.H.A.*

PROVENANCE Royal Dublin Society; acquired by the State 1877 and lodged in The National Museum of Ireland, from where transferred, 1966. N.G.I. 6268.

LITERATURE McGoogan 1915, p. 28, no. 45; Le Harivel 1983, p. 571 (illus.); de Courcy and Maher 1985, p. 34 (illus.).

The interest in topographical, as against pure landscape art, increased in the nineteenth century with the growth of the travel industry, brought about through the invention of the railway and steamship and the burgeoning of a leisured middle class with an appetite for travel. Nicholl was keen to satisfy this market and produced, throughout his career, a very large output of views, both for direct sale to the market, and for translation into engraved form for various publications. This view shows Belfast in the distance, below Cave Hill, viewed from Richard Castle's Newtownbreda Church (1747). Nicholl often painted this aspect; there are two smaller finished watercolours and two studies in the Ulster Museum. The present view dates from late in the artist's career.

RK

ANDREW NICHOLL, R.H.A.

Belfast 1804 - 1886 London

56 Pheasants in a bank of flowers

WATERCOLOUR WITH GOUACHE HIGHLIGHTS ON PAPER 36 x 51.5 cms.

SIGNED lower left, *A. Nicholl R.H.A.*

PROVENANCE Purchased from Mr H.J. Fitzpatrick, Dublin, 1976. N.G.I. 7770.

EXHIBITED Columbus, Toledo and St Louis 1974 (42); Dallas 1976 (39).

LITERATURE Harbison, Potterton and Sheehy 1978, p. 212, plate 33; Le Harivel 1983, p. 572 (illus.); Gillespie, Mooney and Ryan 1986, p. 32 (illus.); Anglesea 1989, p. 84; Butler 1990, p. 79, fig. 75.

Though Nicholl is best known as a topographical painter, he was also a talented painter of flowers and plants. Probably beginning in the 1830s, he created a novel form of composition combining both recognisable views, such as Derry (N.G.I. 7769) with frieze of flowers in the foreground. This was a skill he had the opportunity to perfect while in Ceylon, painting the exotic plant life he found there. The present composition is a variation on this theme, with in this instance, the spray of flowers composed of poppies, marigolds and daisies, which almost obscure two pheasants. The signature suggests that it was painted after the artist was elected a member of the R.H.A. in 1860, but these letters were sometimes added later to his watercolours. Nicholl rarely dated his work.

RK

JAMES GEORGE O'BRIEN

fl. Dublin 1779 - 1819 London

O'Brien studied at the Dublin Society's Schools winning a medal for landscape in 1779. In 1780 he exhibited with the Society of Artists in South William Street. Several of his landscape drawings were engraved for Grose's **The Antiquities of Ireland** *(1791-95). He left Dublin in 1798 and went to London. Returning in 1801 calling himself Oben, a more fashionable Germanic sounding name, he caused some confusion when he contributed to the exhibition held in the Parliament House. He exhibited seventy watercolour views at his own house, 49 Marlborough Street, in 1809. Later that year he went back to London, exhibiting views of Ireland, the north of England and Wales at the Royal Academy from 1810-16.*

57 Vale of Beddgelert, near Mount Snowdon, Wales, 1796

INK AND WATERCOLOUR ON PAPER 38.7 x 56.2 cms.

SIGNED AND DATED in lower left, *J.G. O'Brien 1796*

INSCRIBED AND SIGNED in lower right, *Vale of Bethyellam North Wales J.G. O'Brien Dublin*

PROVENANCE Professor G.F. Mitchell, County Louth, by whom presented, December 1986. N.G.I. 19,334.

EXHIBITED Dublin 1988 (69).

This is a renowned beauty spot in North Wales. Before the inscription identifying the locale was found, it was believed to be just a picturesque view with its fisherman, mill and insubstantial bridge set over a fast moving river. In fact this area around Mount Snowdon was much favoured by artists in search of the sublime without travelling to the Alps. George Barret and Richard Wilson were the first notable artists there, with Turner visiting later in the 1790s and George Grattan around 1800. O'Brien exhibited several Welsh views at the Dublin Parliament House in 1801.

There is a particularly delicate use of colour in this work by him. He has also utilised the black ink for definition in important areas, rather than just colouring in an outline drawing as was the typical method of the time.

MW

WILLIAM ORPEN, R.H.A.

Stillorgan 1878 - 1931 *London*

Sir William Orpen was one of the leading Edwardian society portrait painters. His output was extraordinary and he was one of the highest paid artists of his day. An exceptional student, he studied at the Metropolitan School of Art, Dublin, from 1891 and later at the Slade School of Fine Art, London (1897-99). In 1901 he married Grace Knewstub in Highgate, and the following year he opened a School of Art in Chelsea with Augustus John. He began exhibiting with the New English Art Club in 1906, and from 1908 at the Royal Academy. In 1908 also he was elected a full Academician of the Royal Hibernian Academy, from which he resigned in 1915 under the Presidency of Dermod O'Brien. With his natural interest in people, and instinctive feel for character Orpen set out during the first decade of this century to establish himself as a portrait painter. In 1917 he was appointed as Official War Artist, and the same perception resulted in the remarkable drawings and paintings of the First World War. The following year there was an exhibition of his war paintings at Agnew's, and Orpen received his Knighthood. In 1919 he was elected as an Academician at the Royal Academy. He published his war memoirs in 1921 (An Onlooker in France), and in 1924 Stories of Old Ireland and Myself. Orpen 'the man' as opposed to 'the artist' was a complex personality. As McConkey has remarked 'Orpen put up a front. He lived at a time when artists, particularly portraitists were socially integrated - when the Court painter was preferred to the bohemian outsider.' (McConkey, 1987, p. 9) Throughout the 1920s he created a character referring to himself in letters and anecdotes in the third person as 'Orpsie boy' or ''ickle Orps', a comic little fellow hardly reconcilable with his position as the leading Society painter, yet his essential protection against that society. He refused to leave London for Ireland, yet he was active in the Irish Cultural Renaissance, and painted many of the leading figures, completing the series begun by John Yeats for the Gallery of Modern Art, opened by Sir Hugh Lane, whose plans he fully supported.

58 A man and woman on a horse, study for 'The Western Wedding', c.1913

BLACK AND RED CHALK, PENCIL AND WATERCOLOUR ON PAPER 74.5 x 62 cms.

SIGNED lower right, *ORPEN*

PROVENANCE Purchased from Knoedler and Co., London, 1933. N.G.I. 2948

EXHIBITED London and New York 1967 (104); Dublin 1978 (192).

LITERATURE White 1967, pp. 411-12; Arnold 1981, p. 292 (illus.); Le Harivel 1983, p. 600 (illus.); Gillespie, Mooney and Ryan 1986, p. 44 (illus.).

This is an unfinished study for the painting **A Western Wedding.** The painting was one of three painted by Orpen between 1913 and 1916 in a new medium which had been developed by Winsor and Newton, the 'marble medium' which resulted in a flat tempera-like finish. The two other works in this medium are **Sowing New Seed** and **The Holy Well** (N.G.I. 4030). All three are further characterised by their subject matter and Orpen's use of symbolism to present his very personal interpretation of Irish society and culture.

This is one of numerous drawings and sketches Orpen made for the painting, some of which were exhibited and sold at the New English and at the Society of Twelve in 1915. The figure of the man, and the horse, are more finished. The woman is barely sketched in. Orpen has slightly indicated the incline of the hillside in the strong yellow background. The drawing is squared up, and he has indicated the eventual 'lt. [left] edge of picture'. He has also written colour notes for himself: 'black shawl' for the woman, 'black' for the horse's reins and 'saddle blue - Donegal'. The figures of the man and woman on horseback change little in the finished painting where they pose somewhat incongrously on top of a rocky knoll. Clutching his black book to his chest, this stocky man with the haughty expression is literally looking down on the scene below, as though he is presiding over this country wedding in a position more powerful even than that of the priest - he is almost indeed, on the level of the roadside crucifix. He may be the matchmaker as suggested by Arnold.

FC

59 Portrait of Oliver Sheppard, 1907

PENCIL ON PAPER 34.9 x 28 cms.

SIGNED top right, *William Orpen. 1907.*

PROVENANCE purchased from Miss Cathleen Sheppard, the sitter's daughter, 1959. N.G.I. 3305.

EXHIBITED Dublin 1965 (67); Dublin 1970 (126); Dublin 1978 (173).

LITERATURE Arnold 1981, p. 162 (illus.); Le Harivel 1983, p. 601 (illus.).

'He was a realist....When he drew and painted people he allowed their personalities to flow over him, not through intellectual exchange, but through the visible evidence which his eyes perceived and his hand set down' (Arnold 1981, p. 7).

Born in County Tyrone, Oliver Sheppard (1864-1931) studied at the Metropolitan School of Art, Dublin, and at South Kensington. He subsequently went to Paris where he spent some time at the Académie Julien. He returned to the Westminster School of Art, before settling in Dublin in 1867. In 1898 he was made an Associate of the Royal Hibernian Academy, and a full Member in 1901. Among the many public monuments he executed is the statue of Cuchulain in the General Post Office. Sheppard was a professor at the Metropolitan of Art, and supported Orpen when Orpen was involved in the 'Inquiry into the work carried on by the Royal Hibernian Academy and the Metropolitan School of Art, Dublin'. Much of Orpen's evidence to the Committee of Inquiry, given in October 1905, criticised his own education at the Metropolitan School and indeed his former headmaster James Brenan. Orpen was outspoken and when the report was published in November 1906 he wrote to Grace: 'There are still rows going on over here over my evidence before the Commission - everybody looks strangely at me - like as if I was some deadly microbe - except Sheppard who is delighted'. With few and rapid strokes Orpen indicates Sheppard's jacket and waistcoat, yet these are sufficient to create the sense that Sheppard is slightly pulling back, probably to hold himself straight in his chair. Orpen was sitting at a slightly lower level with the result that his subject is looking down at him, this pose enforcing his rather tense or anxious expression.

FC

WALTER FREDERICK OSBORNE

Dublin 1859 - 1903 Dublin

*Walter Osborne was the son of William Osborne (1823-1901), a noted animal painter. The father must have looked favourably on his son's aspiration to be an artist as he left school at sixteen to attend classes at the Royal Hibernian Academy, where he developed into a prize pupil, winning the prestigious Taylor Scholarship in 1881. To finish his training, he travelled to Antwerp where he studied at the Academy for eighteen months, in the company of his compatriots Nathaniel Hill and Joseph Malachy Kavanagh, also the Englishman Blandford Fletcher. There, he received a thorough grounding in the technical and academic aspects of painting and acquired the habit of sketching out of doors on trips with his colleagues. From Antwerp he moved to Quimperlé in Brittany where he further developed a taste for **plein air** painting, working under the influence of Jules Bastien-Lepage. Though he returned to Dublin following his sojourn in Brittany, Osborne spent most of the following years, into the early 1890s, working in England, spending the warmer months painting rural and coastal scenes and only returning home to pass the winter months in Dublin. He continued to paint rural scenes when in Ireland, but also showed a particular talent for depicting the Dublin streetscape, painting images of its markets and parks. From about 1893 onwards, possibly due to financial demands, he also painted a number of portraits, including a very fine likeness of Sir Walter Armstrong (N.G.I. 1389), Director of the Gallery from 1892-1914, in whose company he visited France and Spain in 1895 and Holland in 1896. Osborne was elected an A.R.H.A. in 1883 and full Academician in 1886.*

60 The House Builders, 1902

WATERCOLOUR ON PAPER 47.7 x 59.8 cms.

SIGNED AND DATED lower left, *Walter Osborne 1902*

PROVENANCE Purchased from the artist's executors, 1903. N.G.I. 2536

EXHIBITED N.E.A.C. Winter 1902 (14); R.H.A. Memorial Exhibition 1903-04 (173); Dallas 1976 (61); Dublin and Belfast 1983 (75).

LITERATURE Sheehy 1974, no. 571; Le Harivel 1983, p. 604 (illus.); Gillespie, Mooney and Ryan 1986, p. 38; Butler 1990, p. 162, fig. 179.

Among Osborne's most engaging creations are his compositions with children, a subject he treated frequently in watercolour. It is obvious that he found the company of children pleasing and fascinating, and he was skilled in illustrating their childish pastimes and preoccupations. In this intimate work, he has chosen to depict two girls, possibly members of the Reilly family from Portmarnock, totally absorbed in building a house out of a pack of cards. It is a carefree existence, the children shown in a warm and comfortable interior, which has been rendered in a loose impressionistic manner, reflecting the influence of contemorary Continental and English painting.

RK

61 Portrait of John Hughes, 1903

WATERCOLOUR ON PAPER 60.8 x 46.5 cms.

INSCRIBED lower left, *This is my portrait by Walter Osborne. One of the last pictures he painted. Presented by me to Lady Stoker May 1903 John Hughes*

PROVENANCE John Hughes, by whom presented to Lady Stoker; bequeathed by her husband, Sir William Thornley Stoker, 1912. N.G.I. 2668.

EXHIBITED R.H.A. Memorial Exhibition 1903-04 (180); Dublin 1907 (264); London and New York 1967 (98); W.S.I. Centenary Exhibition 1970 (108); Dublin and Belfast 1983 (97).

LITERATURE Strickland 1913, vol. 2, p. 204; Sheehy 1974, no. 583; Le Harivel 1983, p. 606 (illus.).

Apart from his talents as a painter in oils, Osborne was a skilled watercolourist and produced numerous portraits in this medium. According to Stephen Gwynne, he turned to portraiture to cover the increasing costs to his domestic responsibilities following the death of his sister Violet Stockley in 1893. But this could not be the only reason for his interest in portraiture, as the relaxed informality of his paintings of family, friends and professional colleagues make evident. This portrait shows the sculptor John Hughes (1865-1941) working in his studio on the marble of **Orpheus and Eurydice** (1897-1903). The sculpture was exhibited at the 1907 Irish International Exhibition (where the watercolour was also shown) and is today in the Hugh Lane Municipal Gallery of Modern Art. Hughes, who trained in London and Paris, then travelled to Italy, first worked as a teacher in the Plymouth Technical School before returning to Dublin in 1894 when he was appointed instructor in modelling at the Metropolitan School of Art and Professor of Sculpture in the R.H.A. School. His most important commissions were a series of bronze reliefs for Loughrea Cathedral (c.1901) and the **Queen Victoria Memorial** (1903-06), formerly outside Leinster House. From 1903 he lived abroad.

RK

This is my portrait
by Walter Osborne. one of
the last pictures he painted.
Presented by me
to Lady Arthur.
May 1903   Arthur ____

SEÁN O'SULLIVAN, R.H.A.

Dublin 1906 · 1964 Nenagh

*Seán O'Sullivan was a gifted portrait artist. He
was educated at the Christian Brothers' School,
Synge Street, Dublin and studied painting at
the Metropolitan School of Art. He won a
scholarship to London where he studied under
Spencer Pryse and Zarraga at the Central School
of Art. He then went to Paris to study at La
Grande Chaumière and Colarossi's. He returned
to Dublin and began teaching at the
Metropolitan School of Art. His talent as a
draughtsman was appreciated quickly and he
received many commissions for pencil and oil
portraits. In 1928, at the age of twenty-one, he
became the youngest artist ever elected as an
Associate of the Royal Hibernian Academy. He
was elected a full member in 1931. O'Sullivan
was a big, burly man, with a soft heart and a
sensitive feel for his sitters who included
Douglas Hyde, Eamon de Valera, W.B. Yeats
and Sir Alfred Chester Beatty. He was also a
competent landscape painter and
stamp designer.*

62 Portrait of James Joyce, 1935

RED CHALK AND CHARCOAL WITH WHITE HIGHLIGHTS ON GREY PAPER 54.5 x 38 cms.

SIGNED AND DATED lower right, *Seán O Sullivan RHA Paris 1935*

PROVENANCE Purchased from the Dawson Gallery, Dublin, 1950. N.G.I. 3037.

EXHIBITED Dallas 1976 (84).

LITERATURE Le Harivel, 1983, p. 612 (illus.).

Seán O'Sullivan was arguably the most naturally gifted Irish portrait-draughtsman
of this century. His technical facility was superb and his portrait drawings
provide us with a gallery of excellent likenesses of the luminaries of Irish society
over four decades. It has been said of him that it is easier to mention the
distinguished figures he did not paint than those he did. O'Sullivan's oil
portraits and his landscapes are under-rated but it was his speed and sureness of
hand as a portrait draughtsman which won him special admiration.

Following his training at the Metropolitan School of Art, O'Sullivan went to
London on a scholarship and from there to Paris where he met James Joyce
(1882-1941). O'Sullivan shared the great writer's interest in languages and in
modern literature. There are two drawings of Joyce by O'Sullivan in the
collection of the National Gallery of Ireland, both of which are dated 'Paris
1935' (see N.G.I. 3557). In the present drawing, Joyce is shown in three-quarter
profile staring intently to the right. The chalk highlights are used in an efficient
but understated way to focus our attention on the bold outline of the head of
the extraordinary author of **Dubliners, A Portrait of the Artist as Young Man,
Ulysses** and **Finnegan's Wake.**

BPK

Frank D Sullivan ano Paris 1935

SEÁN O'SULLIVAN, R.H.A.

Dublin 1906 · 1964 Nenagh

63 Portrait of John McCormack, 1943

PENCIL ON PAPER 47 x 36.5 cms.

SIGNED AND DATED lower right, *Seán O'Sullivan RHA 1943*

PROVENANCE Purchased from the Dawson Gallery, Dublin, 1963. N.G.I. 3534.

EXHIBITED Dublin 1974 (80).

LITERATURE Cowell 1980, p. 66; Le Harivel, 1983, p. 613 (illus.).

The world-famous operatic and concert tenor Count John McCormack (1884-1945) retired to Dublin in 1942 after a long and strenuous career at the top of his profession. He lived at the Shelbourne Hotel, Dublin, for eighteen months before moving in 1944 to a house on the Rock Road at Booterstown. His career had begun in 1902 when he won the coveted Dublin Feis Ceoil gold medal. It is interesting to note that James Joyce had a good tenor voice and might have won the Feis Ceoil competition in 1904 had he been able to sight read. He strode off the stage in disgust when asked to read a piece and as a result was awarded the silver medal not the gold. Seán O'Sullivan's fine portrait study of Ireland's most celebrated tenor was drawn in 1943. It provides a compassionate and sensitive study of the sitter who gazes at us, his mind lost in other thoughts. His expression is slightly sad, a great singer at the end of his career, whose voice had been severely weakened by constant touring and over five hundred recordings.

BPK

GEORGE PETRIE, P.R.H.A.

Dublin 1789 - 1866 Dublin

*George Petrie was not only an artist, but an antiquarian, writer and a musician. According to William Stokes his friend was 'a man of retiring, studious, and contemplative habits.' (Stokes 1868, p. v). Petrie's father James Petrie was a miniature painter in Dublin, and a numismatist. Petrie began drawing under his father's instruction, later attending the drawing school of the Dublin Society where he met Francis Danby and James Arthur O'Connor both of whom would remain life-long friends. He obtained the Society's silver medal in 1805 for a figure drawing. From an early age, and while on sketching trips, he showed an avid interest in antiquities, recording sites he had seen and commenting on their origins and uses. His accuracy in drawing landscapes and buildings led to his drawings being used as illustrations in many early nineteenth century Irish guide-books. In 1828 he was the first painter working solely in watercolours to be elected a Member of the Royal Hibernian Academy. Almost thirty years later, and amid some controversy, he was elected as President of the R.H.A. He made a valuable contribution to the Royal Irish Academy as he developed the museum and library by securing valuable antiquities for the first, and important Irish manuscripts for the second. He contributed numerous papers to the Academy's Transactions and Proceedings, and also to the **Dublin Penny Journal** (1832-33) and the **Irish Penny Journal** (1840-41). As head of the topographical and historical department of the Ordnance Survey of Ireland (1835-42), Petrie, and a team of Irish scholars, collected information on the antiquities, place-names and local history of the various counties in Ireland. In addition he sought to collect and preserve old Irish music, some of which was published in 1855 as **The Petrie Collection of the Native Music of Ireland.**

64 The Twelve Pins, Connemara, County Galway, from the north, 1831

PENCIL AND WATERCOLOUR WITH GUM ARABIC ON PAPER 29.4 x 41.1 cms.

SIGNED AND DATED lower right, *Geo: Petrie Pinxit. 1831*

ENGRAVED by Newton Fielding, published W.F. Wakeman, Dublin, 1835, (N.G.I. 20,351) and for *Picturesque sketches of some of the finest landscape and coastal scenery in Ireland* (1835).

PROVENANCE Robert Callwell; bequeathed by his daughter, Miss Annie Callwell, 1904. N.G.I. 6027.

LITERATURE Le Harivel 1983, p. 624 (illus.); de Courcy and Maher 1985, p. 40 (illus.).

Petrie has painted a great sweep of land, with a shepherd boy resting in the foreground contemplating the beauty of the landscape stretching far before him to the distant mountains, the Twelve Bens (or Twelve Pins). From the central peak Benbaun (2,290 ft.), a series of ridges radiate, each rising in a number of quartzite peaks. Strickland criticises Petrie's watercolours for their 'prevailing bright crome foreground, and hard, blue, distant background' (Strickland 1913, vol. 2, p. 238) yet Petrie has captured the beauty of these strange, cone-like forms. He laid down a broad biscuit-coloured wash, which he builds on, with broad washes of green, and mauve and purple lower down in the heather covered bogland. Shorter strokes give foreground texture to the tufts of grass and reeds, while the mid-distance and background are more delicately handled. Using alternating areas of sunshine and shadow he creates a fine sense of distance. The landscape is sprinkled with little figures; in the face of the grandeur of Nature man is reduced to a number of tiny, bright dots. The Gallery also possesses a preparatory pencil drawing for the Twelve Pins (N.G.I. 6672).

FC

65 Gougane Barra Lake with the Hermitage of
St. Finbarr, County Cork, c.1831

WATERCOLOUR ON PAPER 30.9 x 39.7 cms.

INSCRIBED AND SIGNED lower right, *To my friend R. Callwell by Geo. Petrie. R.H.A.*

PROVENANCE Gift from the artist to Robert Callwell; bequeathed by his daughter, Miss Annie Callwell, 1904. N.G.I. 6028

EXHIBITION R.H.A. 1831 (226); Dublin 1853 (1010); Dallas 1976 (31); Dublin 1980 (15).

LITERATURE Le Harivel 1983, p. 625 (illus.); de Courcy and Maher 1985, p. 46 (illus.).

Lough Gougane Barra, the source of the river Lee, is a small deep lake walled in on three sides by precipices, which are enveloped in Petrie's watercolour by dark, threatening clouds. It has been raining, and the mountainsides are veiled by cataracts, highlighted with little blobs of white paint. An eerie light penetrates the clouds, that strange steel grey light that follows a downpour, and it is reflected in the still water and surrounding land, unifying the whole landscape.

Gougane Barra is closely connected with St Finbarr of Cork, the seventh century monk who established his first settlement on the small island, and reputedly drowned a dragon that had been missed by St Patrick. The ruins of what are reputed to be the Saint's original cell and part of the first chapel on the island have long been a place of pilgrimage. It was widely believed that the water had the power to cure all diseases in both animal and man. The focal point in the painting is the small oratory on the island which is connected to the shore by a narrow causeway. A shaft of light pierces the sky and dramatically illuminates this mecca for the many blue and red dotted pilgrims making their way along the lakeshore.

FC

FRANCIS PLACE

Dinsdale 1647 · 1728 York

In accordance with his father's wishes, Francis Place first pursued a career in law, articled to an attorney in Gray's Inn from 1663-65 when he left the city to avoid the plague. His artistic interests benefitted from his acquaintance with the renowned topographical artist and engraver, Wenceslaus Hollar. Though he never considered himself a student of Hollar, there is little doubt that his influence was critical to his activity as an artist. Place began to travel about England in 1668 when Hollar left for Algiers, and his drawings mark the beginnings of his topographical interests. Around 1675, Place settled in York where he became involved with Lord Halifax, William Lodge, merchant Ralph Thoresby and glass painter Henry Gyles, part of the group known as the 'York Virtuosi'. During the 1670s he visited The Netherlands where he must surely have taken the opportunity to acquaint himself more fully with Dutch art. Place pursued a variety of interests including antiquities, ceramics, finance and fishing. In the realm of art his output was equally varied, working in pen and ink, engraving and mezzotint. Apart from his topographical drawings, he also executed numerous still-life subjects of flowers, fish and birds.

66 A view of Dublin from the Phoenix Park, 1698

PEN AND INK WITH COLOURED WASH ON PAPER 27.5 x 45.2 cms. (with vertical fold mark)

INSCRIBED bottom centre, in the artist's hand, *Dublin from the Park beside the house caled the Phonix* [sic.]

PROVENANCE From the artist by direct descent to Patrick Allan-Fraser, through his wife Elizabeth Fraser, the heiress of Hospitalfield, Arbroath; Patrick Allan-Fraser sale, Sotheby's 10 June 1931, lot 135, bought by John Maher, Dublin and bequeathed 1962 to Michael J. Flynn, Dublin; Gerald Kenyon, Dublin; Rose Black, Dublin; Cynthia O'Connor Gallery, Dublin; Leger Galleries, London, from whom purchased, 1972 (Shaw Fund). N.G.I. 7516.

EXHIBITED London 1972 (9); Dublin 1975 (118); Dublin 1988 (-).

LITERATURE Maher 1932, pp. 9-11, no. 11; Moorman 1952, pp. 159-60; Daniels 1972, p. 302; Webber 1972, p. 10; Le Harivel 1983, p. 643 (illus.); Dublin 1983, p. 48, fig. 26a; Igoe and Dwyer 1988, pp. 79 (illus.), 81.

This panorama of Dublin is one of nineteen drawings by Place in the collection, all of which date to the period of his visit to Ireland in 1698-99 (from which more than thirty-six drawings survive). The present work is one of three views in the collection which the artist sketched in this area on the western approach to the city, along the river Liffey, at Islandbridge. The vantage point on Thomas's Hill, in the Phoenix Park, was later chosen by William Ashford for a fine canvas (N.G.I. 4138). The park had been established as a Royal deer park by Charles II in 1662, and been walled in over the period 1664-69. It was opened to the public in 1747. By then, Phoenix House, the country residence of the Lord Lieutenant from where Place made his drawing, had been demolished to build the Magazine Fort. The bridge, which dominates the foreground, was built by Sir Philip Sydney about 1566, when he was Lord Deputy. After rebuilding and flood damage, it was replaced 1793-94 by the present structure. The buildings which are clustered to the right of the bridge include properties owned by Sir William Robinson, the Irish Surveyor-General and architect of the Royal Hospital, and Sir John Temple, the Solicitor-General. That to the rear left, Davies's brewery, was completed just prior to Place's sketch as it appears in an unfinished state in a painting of the same site by Thomas Bate, executed about 1695 (private collection). The large building just to the right of the brewery was known as Mitchell's Folly. It was built by Alderman Michael Mitchell on land leased from Robinson. Just to their right, but not represented in the present drawing, should be the Royal Hospital, now home of the Irish Museum of Modern Art, which Place shows in another drawing (N.G.I. 7517). In the distance can be seen the city of Dublin with the wooden bridge in the centre, one of just four bridges which spanned the river at this time.

RK

THOMAS SAUTELL ROBERTS, R.H.A.

Waterford 1760 · 1826 Dublin

Born in Waterford, T.S. Roberts was the younger
brother of Thomas Roberts. In 1777 he began
studying at the Dublin Society Architectural
School and even became apprenticed to
architect Thomas Ivory, before deciding to
become a professional artist. His early oils are
close to his brother's work but with less
softness in the lighting. Before 1800 T.S.
Roberts was primarily a watercolourist. Twelve
aquatints of Irish scenery were published from
his work 1795-99. He exhibited both Irish and
English views at the Royal Academy from 1789-
1811 and also exhibited at the British
Institution from 1807-18. In his later oils there
is a marked affinity for more rugged scenery
than his brother depicted, particularly in views
of the river Dargle. He was nominated with
William Ashford and William Cuming to choose
the first Academicians for the Royal Hibernan
Academy and himself exhibited five oils and
two watercolours at the first exhibition in 1826.

67 View of the countryside near Bray, County Wicklow, looking towards Killiney Bay, 1793

WATERCOLOUR OVER INK AND PENCIL ON PAPER 25.7 x 37.5 cms.

SIGNED AND DATED lower right, T.S. Roberts -93.

INSCRIBED below, on original mount, View of the Country near Bray, County of Dublin

PROVENANCE Christie's, London, 15 June 1982, lot 23, bought by Hartley Fine Arts, London, from whom purchased, 1982. N.G.I. 18,991.

EXHIBITED Dublin 1983 (52).

LITERATURE Le Harivel 1983, p. 662 (illus.); Gillespie, Mooney and Ryan 1986, p. 8 (illus.).

This attractive watercolour depicts the coastline to the north of Bray, County Wicklow (beyond the tree on the right), looking towards Killiney Bay and Hill. On the latter, the well known obelisk, erected by Colonel John Mapas can be seen. He lived nearby at Mount Mapas (today known as Killiney Castle) and sought to provide work for unemployed labourers in 1742. Many artists came to sketch along the river Dargle from Bray to the Powerscourt Estate and this panorama was often painted, for instance by John Henry Campbell (N.G.I. 6342).

Although there are two other works on paper by T.S. Roberts in the collection they show other facets of his style. *The Four Courts and River Liffey from Usher's Quay* (N.G.I. 2439) is a detailed outline pencil drawing for an aquatint, while *Curraghmore House, Portlaw, County Waterford* (N.G.I. 7881) is less detailed than the present work, showing a distant view of a house remodelled by the artist's father, John Roberts. T.S. Roberts' work in oil is not always as fine as his brother's but as this example shows he was a master of the small scale watercolour with well painted trees and able to convey the spaciousness of the view. His colour and picturesque foreground figures place him the in the 18th century tradition of landscape painting. This is one of only a few signed works prior to 1800 which are known by him. He may have intended to engrave it.

MW

HENRY TRESHAM, R.A.

Dublin 1750/51 - 1814 London

*Tresham studied with Jacob Ennis, and with Robert West, at the Dublin Society Schools. In 1775 he left home and after a brief sojourn in London went to Italy, settling in Rome. He became a noted member of the emigré artistic community. Tresham soon became quite prominent as a dealer, including among his clientele Frederick Hervey, Bishop of Derry. When the latter succeeded his brother as Earl of Bristol, in 1780, Tresham saw fit to give a large party. Few of Tresham's paintings are known at present; those which have survived are rather vapid. However, some must have been impressive since, following his return to London, in 1789, he exhibited at the Royal Academy was elected to full membership, and, in 1807, appointed the Academy's Professor of Painting. This latter post he resigned in 1809, but continued to act as dealer, and to paint. A very fine portrait of Tresham survives, showing him with Canova admiring Canova's **Cupid and Psyche,** in the sculptor's studio. This group is in pastel by another Irishman, Hugh Douglas Hamilton, and is in private ownership.*

68 Lo speco della divinatrice, c.1784

INK WITH BROWN WASH 23.2 x 18.7 cms.

ENGRAVED by Tresham for **Le avventure di Sappho** (Rome 1784), p. 10.

PROVENANCE Purchased from Heim Gallery, London, 1975. N.G.I. 7760.

EXHIBITED London 1975 (107) as by Jacques Réattu.

LITERATURE Le Harivel 1983, p. 696 (illus.); Figgis 1988, p. 129 (illus.).

In the latter part of the eighteenth century, there was a considerable revival of interest in the person and work of this ancient Greek poetess. Somewhat later she became a heroine for lady authors. Tresham did a total of eighteen engravings for **Le avventure di Sappho,** following closely the Italian text of Alessandro Verri, published in 1780.

The title of this drawing comes from the inscription on the engraving which, roughly translated, reads: 'The cave of the soothsayer. Sappho was perplexed, divided between obedience and fear of the unknown rite'. On the *verso* is a **Procession before a classical temple**, executed in pen and ink, with grey and green wash. Since this is clearly cut down at both top and left, Tresham intended the *recto* described above to be the primary drawing, which he proceeded to engrave.

MW

PATRICK TUOHY, A.R.H.A.

Dublin 1894 - 1930 New York

Patrick Tuohy was the son of a respected Dublin surgeon. His parents were ardent Irish nationalists and they sent him to Patrick Pearse's school, St Enda's, in Rathfarnham. Despite the handicap of being born without a left hand, the art teacher, the sculptor, William Pearse (Patrick's brother), recognised Tuohy's drawing ability and encouraged him to attend night classes at the Metropolitan School of Art.

He studied there under Orpen and won the Taylor Art Scholarship in 1912 and in 1915. He went to Spain the following year and visited the Prado regularly, where he was influenced by the great Spanish painters, especially Velázquez and Zurbarán. He first exhibited at the Royal Hibernian Academy in 1918 and also began teaching at the Metropolitan School of Art. He was elected an Associate of the R.H.A. in 1926. He completed a number of religious commissions and many portraits. In 1927, Tuohy emigrated to the United States of America having become disillusioned about his career prospects in Ireland. He went to South Carolina that year and then settled in New York.

Tuohy was a complex personality, at times witty but also moody and subject to bouts of depression. Just as he began to win the attention of American critics, tragically, in August 1930, he took his own life. His body was returned to Ireland and he was buried at Glasnevin Cemetery, Dublin.

69 Supper Time, 1912

PENCIL AND WATERCOLOUR WITH WHITE HIGHLIGHTS ON PAPER 50 x 70 cms.

PROVENANCE Purchased from Miss Bride Tuohy, the artist's sister, Dublin, 1959. N.G.I. 3306.

LITERATURE Le Harivel, 1983, p. 698 (illus.); Gillespie, Mooney and Ryan, 1986, p. 45 (illus.); Mulcahy 1989-90, p. 110.

Supper Time won Patrick Tuohy the Taylor Art Scholarship in 1912. It is a wonderfully executed watercolour and an auspicious debut for an eighteen-year-old artist, 'an exercise in light and reflections - the polished table, silver vessels and the window were vehicles for the young painter to show his virtuosity' (Mulcahy 1989-90, p. 110). But the picture is also perhaps a psychological drama. A woman sits in the centre pouring milk into a cup, with a young boy, laughing, seated on her right, and to her left a slightly older girl is reading intently from a book placed on the table. On the near side of the table, to the right, a middle aged man is seen from the side, only partially, his face in profile. There are reflections in the small paned window behind the group. But whose is the mysterious face in the window?

There is something distinctly odd about this scene. Why are there only two cups when there are four people seated at the table? Why are there so few plates? Why is the man exiled to one side as if he should not really be there? The table cloth has been laid so as to exclude him. Is this really a family group? What should be a mundane occasion, afternoon tea, is weighed heavily with tension and unexplained circumstance. The dramatic light is impressive, sharpening into focus the features of each individual. It creates lively shapes on the table and in the reflections on the silver ware. The colours are strong but tending towards the sombre, adding to the overall psychological effect of this minor masterpiece.

BPK

FRANCIS WHEATLEY, R.A.

London 1747 · 1801 London

Wheatley trained in Shipley's Drawing School, London; later he studied with Richard Wilson. About 1779 he came to Ireland, fleeing creditors, and bringing as his 'wife' a certain Mrs Gresse. At this time Volunteers were being established by notable members of the aristocracy, the Duke of Leinster, Frederick Hervey, Bishop of Derry and Earl of Bristol, Lords Aldborough, Charlemont, among them. The parades of these gave Wheatley plenty of scope for his redoubtable talents, and he was also commissioned to paint important family groups. His **Interior of the Irish House of Commons** (Leeds City Art Gallery), with Henry Grattan speaking, is a most historic picture, not merely as a work of art, but also as a record of a building which, by order, was structurally dismantled following the Act of Union in 1801, while his famous **Dublin Volunteers on College Green** (N.G.I. 125) is equally historic. A number of art historians believe that Wheatley painted many of his best pictures during his Irish sojourn; the same can be said of his watercolours, a medium in which he showed great mastery. In Ireland Wheatley managed to incur debts, and this fact, combined with the discovery of the real status of his 'wife', saw him reversing across the Irish Sea in 1783. In his four short years in Ireland he created a very significant number of works of art of quality and style.

70 The Entry of the Speaker into the Irish House of Commons, 1782

WATERCOLOUR OVER INK ON PAPER 49.7 x 63.8 cms.

SIGNED AND DATED lower right, F. Wheatley del: 1782

PROVENANCE Purchased at Christie's, 11 March 1932, lot 66. N.G.I. 2930.

EXHIBITED London and New York 1967 (65); London 1970 (1255); 1975 Dublin (102); Dallas 1976 (7); Paris 1989.

LITERATURE White 1967, pp. 411-12; Webster 1970, pp. 108-09, fig. 153; Guinness 1979, fig. 82; Le Harivel 1983, p. 721 (illus.).

The artist painted the Irish House of Commons, both from without and within, in oils. In this watercolour view, through Edward Lovett Pearce's magnificient 1730s portico, the Speaker is shown making a ceremonial entry, preceded by his Serjeant-at-arms. At this time the Speaker was Edmond Sexton Pery (1719-1806). Pery resigned from this post in 1785 after fourteen years service. Subsequently he was created Viscount Pery of Newtown-Pery in the county of Limerick. Pery was firmly anti-Union and voted against it. The family flourishes to this day, the senior member being The Earl of Limerick.

MW

FRANCIS WHEATLEY, R.A.

London 1747 - 1801 London

71 Fishermen beside the Salmon Leap, Leixlip, County Kildare, 1782

WATERCOLOUR OVER INK ON PAPER 55.8 x 47 cms.

SIGNED AND DATED lower right, *FWheatley del 1782* (F & W in monogram)

PROVENANCE Purchased at Christie's, 1914. N.G.I. 2701.

LITERATURE Webster 1970, pp. 45-47, fig 47; Le Harivel 1983, p. 720 (illus.).

This view of a waterfall on the river Liffey is almost certainly the famous Salmon Leap at Leixlip, County Kildare, seen from a different viewpoint than that usually used, namely from the left bank rather than from the right bank. The frequently painted salmon leap usually shows the broken arch springing from the left bank. This latter view, with nymphs bathing, is the subject of an oil painting by Wheatley in the Mellon Collection.

The rock formation and the drop of the fall give one reason to believe that the waterfall in the watercolour is the Leixlip salmon leap. Of course since the construction of the dam, and the creation of a reservoir behind it, the view has changed significantly.

MW

JACK BUTLER YEATS, R.H.A.

London 1871 · 1957 Dublin

Jack Yeats was the youngest of the four children of the painter, John Butler Yeats, and his wife, Susan Pollexfen. He spent his boyhood years in Sligo with his maternal grandparents and later remarked 'Sligo was my school and the sky above it' (O'Doherty 1957). He studied at a number of art institutions in London and established himself as an illustrator for various journals and publications. He began to paint in watercolours in the late 1890s and it was not until 1910 when he settled in Ireland that he started to paint consistently in oils. His early work is very different in style and technique when compared to the romantic expressionism of his late paintings. He became an associate of the Royal Hibernian Academy in 1915 and a full member the following year. Yeats produced many novels and plays and his paintings have poetic titles and often contain literary references. He was the most successful Irish artist of his generation and is now receiving international acclaim. His friend, the poet Thomas MacGreevy, wrote that Yeats became 'The national painter...the painter who in his work was the consummate expression of the spirit of his own nation at one of the supreme points in its evolution' (MacGreevy 1945, p.10).

72 The Country Shop, c.1912

WATERCOLOUR OVER INK ON CARD 26.6 x 19.5 cms.

SIGNED upper right, *JACK B. YEATS*

PROVENANCE William A. Cadbury, whose executors presented it 1966. N.G.I. 3829.

EXHIBITED Dublin 1914 (-); W.S.I. Centenary Exhibition 1970 (107).

LITERATURE Yeats, 1912 p. 1 (illus.); Sheehy 1980, p. 96, fig. 85; Le Harivel, 1983, p. 728 (illus.); Pyle 1986, pp. 28-29 (illus.); Gillespie, Mooney and Ryan 1986, p. 42 (illus.); Butler, 1990, p. 198, fig. 226.

Jack Yeats first established himself as an illustrator for various journals and publications. His style of drawing was characterised by a strong sense of line, careful composition and conservative colouring. His aim was to immerse himself in the Irish experience. He remarked: 'We must look to ourselves for the springs of our art...those painters who have the greatest affection for their own country will paint them best' (Capuchin 1945-46, p. 110).

Yeats was particularly fascinated by life in the West of Ireland. In 1905, he toured the poorest districts of the West providing illustrations for John Millington Synge's articles for **The Manchester Guardian**. In 1912, Yeats published a book, **Life in the West of Ireland,** which sought to illustrate the traditional folk life of Sligo and Mayo. **The Country Shop** is the first illustration in this charming book. Yeats details the contents of a local shop, item by item, recording carefully the nutmeg, oils, boots, rope and brushes. The sour-faced shop owner dominates the scene as she scans her account book for the appropriate amount to be charged to the hooded old lady who stands before her clutching her purse. A man on the right looks away but has his ear cocked to the proceedings. This introspective observer appears in many of his later oil paintings.

BPK

JACK BUTLER YEATS, R.H.A.

London 1871 · 1957 Dublin

73 The Circus Chariot, c.1910

CRAYON AND WATERCOLOUR ON PAPER 25.4 x 35.5 cms.

SIGNED lower right, JACK B YEATS; lower left J and JBY (in monogram)

INSCRIBED on verso, A CIRCUS CHAIRIOT (sic).

PROVENANCE Mrs Nancy Pulvertaft; Victor Waddington, London, from whom purchased, 1967. N.G.I. 6316.

EXHIBITED Dublin 1910 (5); London 1967 (1); Bedford 1967 (11A); Dublin and New York 1971 (24); Columbus, Toledo and St Louis 1974 (69); Dallas 1976 (66).

LITERATURE Le Harivel, 1983, p. 728 (illus.); Pyle 1986, pp. 22-23 (illus.); Butler, 1990, p. 198, fig. 200.

The circus was a lifelong passion of Jack Yeats. During his boyhood years which he spent in Ireland, from 1879 to 1887, he loved to visit the circus every time it came to Sligo. After his return to London to live with his parents at Earls Court, he saw Buffalo Bill at the American Exhibition and often visited Sanger's Circus.

The Circus Chariot dates to about 1910, the year in which it was first exhibited. There is one other drawing of a similar subject, The Charioteer, which was drawn in black and white for the September 1908 issue of A Broadside, Yeats's sheet of ballads, poems and illustrations. In Ah Well (1942, p.12), Yeats described chariot races in a circus tent under a long glass roof, and the way the outer wheels used to spray up the sand and dust when the driver spun his team at the turn. The Circus Chariot is obviously a reference to an exciting circus act witnessed in his youth but Yeats transforms it into an ancient chariot race with the piebald horses chasing forward through wind and rain. The watercolour is laid on thickly and the heavy colours enhance the drama of the scene.

BPK

JOHN BUTLER YEATS, R.H.A.

Tullylish, Co. Down 1839 - 1922 New York

John Butler Yeats was a talented portrait painter, and father of a brilliant family, William, the poet, Jack the painter, and Elizabeth ('Lollie') and Susan ('Lily'), the founders of the Dun Emer Industries and its successor, the Cuala Industries. His own father was a Protestant rector in County Down. He was educated at Liverpool and on the Isle of Man. He read metaphysics and logic at Trinity College, Dublin, before studying law. He practised as a barrister until 1867 when he moved to London and enrolled at Heatherley's Art School and then at the Royal Academy School. He returned to Dublin in 1880 but went back to London in 1897. His wife, Susan, died in 1900 and the following year he returned to Dublin again and showed forty-four works in an important joint exhibition with Nathaniel Hone the Younger. The success of this exhibition which was organised by the indomitable Sarah Purser, brought Yeats commissions and, during the next seven years, he painted many of the distinguished Irish men and women of his day. In 1908 he emigrated to the United States of America where he became a much-liked member of the artistic community in New York. He remained there for the rest of his life earning his living by lecturing, writing and painting portraits.

74 Portrait of William Butler Yeats, 1898

PENCIL AND WASH WITH WHITE HIGHLIGHTS ON PAPER 35.6 x 25.3 cms.

SIGNED AND DATED centre right, *J.B. Yeats 1898*

PROVENANCE Purchased at Lady Gregory sale, Coole Park, 1932. N.G.I. 2942.

EXHIBITED Dublin 1965 (3); Dallas 1976 (53).

LITERATURE Le Harivel, 1983, p. 730 (illus.).

The pencil sketch was John Butler Yeats's best working method. He tended to complete his sketches in a single sitting, unlike his oil portraits which he reworked interminably and often to their detriment.

William Butler Yeats, (1865-1939), the eldest son of John Butler Yeats, was a rather weak-looking, bookish man, aged thirty-three, when he sat for this pencil drawing in 1898. In that year, W.B. developed a strong friendship with Lady Augusta Gregory and she began to favour his father with commissions for pencil sketches. W.B.'s health was poor at this time. He was suffering from nervous strain and weak eyesight. This is apparent from his father's taut and well-worked drawing. We sense that the poet is eager to rise from his chair. He stares dreamily into space, his little spectacles, thin face, carefully parted hair and slender, long hands giving the impression of a highly-cultivated but absent-minded man. John Butler Yeats hoped that W.B. would concentrate more on his poetry and less on the theatre. He thought Lady Gregory was distracting his son by involving him in her theatrical projects. 'Had you stayed with me and not left me for Lady Gregory, and her friends and associations, you would have loved and adored concrete life for which as I know you have a real affection' (Yeats 1944, letter no. 229).

BPK

75 Pippa Passes, 1869-72

GOUACHE ON PAPER 48.4 x 34.6 cms.

PROVENANCE Dr John Todhunter; presented by Mr A.C. Hunt, 1962. N.G.I. 3531.

EXHIBITED Dudley Gallery 1871; Dublin 1873 (620); Dublin 1901 (71); Dublin 1965 (92); Cork 1971 (135).

LITERATURE Pyle 1970, p. 10; Murphy 1978, pp. 68-69, 116; Albany 1978, pp. 12, 13 21-22 (illus.) 29; Le Harivel, 1983, p. 732 (illus.); Gillespie, Mooney and Ryan, 1986, p. 36 (illus.); Butler, 1990, p. 164, fig. 184.

Pippa Passes is the title of a dramatic poem written by Robert Browning in 1841 as part of a series titled *Bells and Pomegranates.* As Pippa walks by singing, her songs prevent four crimes. When John Butler Yeats's gouache was exhibited in Dublin in 1873, the catalogue cited the following lines from Browning's poem:

'But let the sun shine! Wherefore repine?
With thee to lead me, O day of mine,
Down the grass path, grey and dew,
Under the pine wood, blind with boughs,
Where the swallow never flew
Nor yet cicala dared carouse -
No, dared carouse.'

Yeats was commissioned to paint *Pippa Passes* in 1869 by his friend, John Todhunter, for a fee of ten pounds. It took three years until 1872 to complete, because Yeats was constantly reworking it, even after it was first exhibited. Pippa's face shows the signs of this but the picture is, nonetheless, a very successful one. It was originally laid down on a wooden panel but this was removed in 1972 (inscribed on the panel under the paper was the name of Yeats' sister-in-law, Isabella Pollexfen). In *Pippa Passes,* Yeats comes closest to the ideal of the Pre-Raphaelites, especially Dante Gabriel Rossetti. While he was a student at the Royal Academy Schools, Yeats and a group of friends contemplated resurrecting the ideas of the Pre-Raphaelite Brotherhood. In 1871, Yeats' exhibited *Pippa Passes* at the Dudley Gallery, London. Rossetti is said to have admired the picture and Browning also enthused about it. The picture shows the influence of Rossetti in the focus on a languid young woman and the dramatic moment as she appears through the trees in her colourful dress. The flow of her figure, the knarled tree trunks and the swirling leaves create a great sense of movement. Cullen has proposed plausibly that *Pippa Passes* shows the influence of *Danaë in the Brazen Chamber* by Frederick Sandys. This sensuous picture of a standing female who holds her hair back like Pippa was painted in 1867 and Yeats could well have seen it on his visits to Sandys' studio in 1867 and 1868. The National Gallery of Ireland has a charcoal drawing (N.G.I. 3253, signed and dated 1871, 35 x 38 cms) which is a preparatory sketch for the head of Pippa. She stares more directly at the viewer than in the final composition.

BPK

Albany 1978

The Drawings of John Butler Yeats 1839-1922,
Albany Institute of History and Art, 1978. Exh. cat. by Fintan Cullen.

Anglesea 1989

Martyn Anglesea,
Portraits and Prospects, British and Irish drawings and watercolours
from collection of The Ulster Museum, Belfast,
(Belfast 1989).

Arnold 1981

Bruce Arnold,
Orpen, Mirror to an Age,
(London 1981).

Bedford 1967

Artists and Architecture of Bedford Park 1875-1900,
St Michael's Vicarage, Bedford, 1967.

Bodkin 1909

Thomas Bodkin, 'R.H.A. Review'
Freeman's Journal,
31 March 1909, p. 5.

Bodkin 1920

Thomas Bodkin,
Four Irish Landscape Painters,
(Dublin 1920).

Bordeaux 1977

La Peinture Britannique de Gainsborough à Bacon,
Galerie des Beaux-Arts, Bordeaux, 1977.

Bourke 1987

Marie Bourke,
The Aran Fisherman's drowned child by Frederic William Burton R.H.A.,
(Dublin 1987).

Bourke 1988

Marie Bourke,
'The Aran Fisherman's drowned child',
GPA Irish Arts Review Yearbook 1988, pp. 190-96.

Bowe 1983

Nicola Gordon Bowe,
Harry Clarke: his graphic art,
(Dublin 1983).

Bowe 1987

Nicola Gordon Bowe, 'Wilhelmina Geddes',
Irish Arts Review,
vol. 4, no. 4, (Autumn 1987), pp. 53-59.

Bowe 1989

Nicola Gordon Bowe,
The Life and Work of Harry Clarke,
(Dublin 1989).

Nicola Gordon Bowe,
'Irish Arts and Crafts Movement 1886-1925',
GPA Irish Arts Review Yearbook 1990-91,
pp. 172-85.

Bowe 1990-91

Nicola Gordon Bowe, David Caron and Michael Wynne,
Gazetteer of Irish Stained Glass.
The works of Harry Clarke and the artists of An Túr Gloine,
(The Tower of Glass) 1903-1963,
(Blackrock, Co. Dublin 1988).

Bowe, Caron and Wynne 1988

Patricia Butler,
Three Hundred Years of Irish Watercolours and Drawings,
(London 1990).

Butler 1990

'Quotations from Jack Yeats',
The Capuchin Annual,
1945-46, p. 110

Capuchin 1945-46

Master European Drawings from
the Collection of the National Gallery of Ireland,
Ackland Art Museum, University of North Carolina;
Colorado Springs Fine Arts Center;
Art Gallery, University of Maryland;
Milwaukee Art Museum;
The Pierpont Morgan Library, New York;
Indianapolis Museum of Art; The Minneapolis Institute of Arts;
The Santa Barbara Museum of Art, 1983.
Exh. cat. by Raymond Keaveney.

North Carolina etc. 1983

Aspects of Irish Art,
Columbus Gallery of Fine Arts,
Toledo Museum of Arts and St Louis Art Museum, 1974.
'A century and a half of Irish painting' exh. cat. entries by James White.

Columbus, Toledo and St Louis 1974

Irish Art in the 19th Century, ROSC '71,
Crawford Municipal School of Art, Cork 1971.
Exh. cat. by Cyril Barrett.

Cork 1971

Rose Barton R.W.S. (1856-1929),
Crawford Municipal Art Gallery, Cork;
Fine Art Society, London;
Ulster Museum, Belfast and Kilkenny Castle, 1987.
Exh. cat. by Charles Nugent and Rebecca Rowe.

Cork, London, Belfast and Kilkenny 1987

de Courcy and Maher 1985   Catherine de Courcy and Ann Maher,
National Gallery of Ireland: Fifty views of Ireland,
(Dublin 1985).

Cowell 1980   John Cowell,
Where they lived in Dublin,
(Dublin 1980).

Craig 1952   Maurice Craig,
Dublin 1660-1860,
(London 1952).

Craig 1984   Maurice Craig,
Georgian Dublin,
(Dublin 1984).

Crookshank 1979   Anne Crookshank,
Irish Art from 1600,
(Dublin 1979).

Crookshank and Glin 1978   Anne Crookshank and The Knight of Glin,
The Painters of Ireland,
(London 1978).

Dallas 1976   **Irish Watercolours 1675-1925 from the National Gallery of Ireland,**
Museum of Fine Arts, Dallas 1976.
Exh. cat. by James White.

Daniels 1972   Jeffrey Daniels, 'Agnew's annual exhibition of English watercolours',
Connoisseur,
vol. 181, (December 1972), p. 302.

D.N.B. 1901   **Dictionary of National Biography XXII, supplement,**
(London 1901).

Dublin 1813   **Society of Artists of the City of Dublin,**
Dublin Society's House, Hawkins Street, fourth annual exhibition, 1813.

Dublin 1853   **Irish Industrial Exhibition,**
Exhibition building, Leinster Lawn, Dublin, 1853.
Exh. cat. by Samuel Sproule.

Dublin 1865   **Dublin International Exhibition of Arts and Manufactures,**
Exhibition Hall, Earlsfort Terrace, Dublin, 1865.

Loan Museum of Art Treasures, Dublin,
Dublin Industrial Exhibition Palace, 1873.

Dublin 1873

Loan Collection of works by Sir Frederic William Burton R.H.A.,
National Gallery of Ireland, Dublin, 1900.

Dublin 1900

Jack B. Yeats: Pictures of Life in the West of Ireland,
Leinster Hall, Dublin, 1910.

Dublin 1910

Black and White Artists Society of Ireland,
Dublin, 1914.

Dublin 1914

Evie Hone 1894-1955,
University College, Dublin, 1958.
Exh. cat. by James White.

Dublin 1958

W.B. Yeats, a Centenary Exhibition,
National Gallery of Ireland, Dublin, 1965.
Exh. cat. by James White and Michael Wynne.

Dublin 1965

Irish Portraits 1660-1860,
National Gallery of Ireland, Dublin;
National Portrait Gallery, London;
Ulster Museum Belfast, 1969-70.
Exh. cat. by Anne Crookshank and The Knight of Glin.

Dublin, London and Belfast 1969-70

The Irish 1870-1970,
National Gallery of Ireland, Dublin, 1970.
Exh. cat. by James White.

Dublin 1970

The Architecture of Ireland in drawings and paintings,
National Gallery of Ireland, Dublin, 1975.
Exh. cat. by various authors.

Dublin 1975

William Orpen, 1878-1931, a Centenary Exhibition,
National Gallery of Ireland, Dublin, 1978.
Exh. cat. by Vera Ryan, John Hutchinson and James White.

Dublin 1978

Harry Clarke,
Douglas Hyde Gallery, Dublin, 1979.
Exh. cat. by Nicola Gordon Bowe.

Dublin 1979

The Early Celtic Revival,
National Gallery of Ireland, Dublin, 1980.
Exh. cat. by Jeanne Sheehy.

Dublin 1980

Dublin 1982

Acquisitions 1981-82,
National Gallery of Ireland, Dublin, 1982.
Exh. cat. by Michael Wynne and Homan Potterton.

Dublin 1983

Acquisitions 1982-83,
National Gallery of Ireland, Dublin, 1983.
Exh. cat. by Adrian Le Harivel and Michael Wynne.

Dublin and Belfast 1983-84

Walter Osborne,
National Gallery of Ireland, Dublin and Ulster Museum, Belfast, 1983-84.
Exh. cat. by Jeanne Sheehy.

Dublin and Belfast 1984

The Irish Impressionists,
National Gallery of Ireland, Dublin and Ulster Museum, Belfast, 1984.
Exh. cat. by Julian Campbell.

Dublin 1984

Antique Dealers Fair/Adam Buck,
Cynthia O'Connor Gallery, Dublin, 1984.

Dublin 1987

Irish Women Artists,
National Gallery of Ireland, Dublin, 1987.
Exh. cat. entries on Barton by Rebecca Rowe and Frances Gillespie;
on Butler by Wanda Ryan.

Dublin 1988

Dublin depicted: a millennium celebration,
National Gallery of Ireland, 1988.
No catalogue; selected and labelled by Susan Dillon.

Dublin 1988a

Acquisitions 1986-1988,
National Gallery of Ireland, Dublin, 1988.
Burton exh. cat. entries by Fionnuala Croke and Adrian Le Harivel.

Dublin 1991

Maurice MacGonigal, R.H.A., 1900-1979,
Hugh Lane Municipal Gallery of Modern Art, Dublin, 1991.
Exh. cat. by Katharine Crouan.

Eastlake 1895

Lady Eastlake,
Journals and Correspondence,
vol. I, (London 1895).

Edinburgh 1985

The Dublin Arts and Crafts Movement 1885-1930,
Edinburgh College of Art and Design, 1985.
Exh. cat. by Nicola Gordon Bowe.

Nicola Figgis, 'Irish Portrait and Subject Painters in Rome 1750-1800', *The GPA Irish Arts Review Yearbook 1988*, pp. 125-36.

Figgis 1988

Stella Frost (Ed.), *Evie Hone*, (Dublin 1958).

Frost 1958

Frances Gillespie, Kim-Mai Mooney and Wanda Ryan, *National Gallery of Ireland: Fifty Irish Drawings and Watercolours*, (Dublin 1986).

Gillespie, Mooney and Ryan 1986

Desmond Guinness, *Georgian Dublin*, (London 1979).

Guinness 1979

G. Haight, *The George Eliot Letters*, vol. 4, (London 1955).

Haight 1955

Peter Harbison, *Guide to the National Monuments in the Republic of Ireland*, (Dublin 1970).

Harbison 1970

Peter Harbison, Homan Potterton and Jeanne Sheehy, *Irish Art and Architecture*, (London 1978)

Harbison, Potterton and Sheehy

Kathryn Moore Heleniak, *William Mulready*, (New Haven and London 1980).

Heleniak 1980

Vivien Igoe and Frederick O'Dwyer, 'Early views of the Royal Hospital Kilmainham', *The GPA Irish Arts Review Yearbook 1988*, pp. 78-88.

Igoe and O'Dwyer 1988

Irish Exhibition of Living Art, annual exhibitions from 1943.

I.E.L.A.

Irische Kunst des Gegenwart, Iserlohn, 1955.

1955 Iserlohn

S.B. Kennedy, *Paul Henry (Lives of Irish Artists)*, (Dublin 1991).

Kennedy 1991

Le Harivel 1983   Adrian Le Harivel (Comp.),
                         National Gallery of Ireland:
                         Illustrated Summary Catalogue of Drawings,
                         Watercolours and Miniatures,
                         (Dublin 1983).

London 1896   **Loan Collection of Water Colour Drawings,**
                         Guildhall, London, 1896.

London 1907   **Irish International Exhibition,**
                         Guildhall, London, 1907.

London 1913   **Whitechapel Exhibition of Irish Art,**
                         Whitechapel Gallery, London, 1913.

London 1959   **Evie Hone 1894-1955,**
                         The Arts Council Gallery and Tate Gallery, London, 1959.
                         Exh. cat. by James White.

London 1967   **Jack B. Yeats: early drawings and watercolours,**
                         Victor Waddington, London, 1967.

London and New York 1967 **Drawings from the National Gallery of Ireland,**
                         Wildenstein, London and New York, 1967.
                         Exh. cat. by Denys Sutton.

London 1970   **The Age of Neo-Classicism,**
                         Royal Academy, London, 1970.
                         Exh. cat. by numerous writers.

London 1972   **Daniel Maclise 1806-1870,**
                         National Portrait Gallery, London, 1972.
                         Exh. cat. by Richard Ormond and John Turpin.

London 1972a   **English Watercolours,**
                         Leger Galleries, London, 1972.

London 1975   **Exhibition of French drawings: Neo-classicism,**
                         Heim Gallery, London, 1975.

London 1987   **Orpen and the Edwardian Era,**
                         Pyms Gallery, London, 1987.
                         Exh. cat. by Kenneth McConkey.

Ada K. Longfield, 'Samuel Dixon's embossed pictures of flowers and birds',
Irish Georgian Society Bulletin,
vol. 18, no. 4. (October-December 1975), pp. 109-36.

Longfield 1975

Eileen MacCarvill (Ed.),
Mainie Jellett the Artist's vision,
(Dundalk 1958).

MacCarvill 1958

A. McGoogan,
National Museum of Science and Art:
Catalogue of Water-Colour and Oil Paintings, Chalk and Pencil Drawings etc.,
(Dublin 1915).

McGoogan 1915

Jane MacFarlane,
Sir Frederic William Burton R.H.A.: his Life and Work, B.A. Thesis,
Trinity College Dublin, 1976.

MacFarlane 1976

Thomas MacGreevy,
Jack B. Yeats: an Appreciation and an interpretation,
(Dublin 1945).

MacGreevy 1945

Edward McParland,
James Gandon, Vitruvius Hibernicus,
(London 1985).

McParland 1985

John Maher,
'Francis Place in Dublin',
Journal of the Royal Society of Antiquaries of Ireland,
(1932), pp. 1-14.

Maher 1932

Huon Mallalieu,
The Dictionary of British Watercolour Painters up to 1920,
2 vols., (Woodbridge 1979).

Mallalieu 1979

Huon Mallalieu,
The Dictionary of British Watercolour Painters up to 1920,
vol. 3, (Woodbridge 1990).

Mallalieu 1990

Royal Jubilee Exhibition,
Manchester, 1887.

Manchester 1887

Theo Moorman,
'Some newly discovered drawings by Francis Place',
Burlington Magazine,
vol. 94, (June 1952), pp. 159-60.

Moorman 1952

Mulcahy 1989-90

Rosemarie Mulcahy,
'Patrick J. Tuohy 1894-1930',
The GPA Irish Arts Review Yearbook 1989-90,
pp. 107-18.

Murphy 1978

William M. Murphy,
Prodigal Father: the Life of John Butler Yeats,
(Cornell University 1978).

N.G.I. 1990

National Gallery of Ireland,
(London 1990).
Guide by Raymond Keaveney, Michael Wynne,
Adrian Le Harivel and Fionnuala Croke.

N.E.A.C.

New English Art Club, London,
exhibitions from 1886-1925.

O'Brien 1920

Dermod O'Brien,
'Catalogue of pictures, sketches and studies by Nathaniel Hone, R.H.A.,
in the collection of Mrs Hone at the time of her death',
in Thomas Bodkin, op. cit.

O'Doherty 1957

Brian O'Doherty,
'Jack B. Yeats (obituary)',
The Dublin Magazine,
vol. 32, no. 3, July 1957.

O'Keefe and Simington 1991

Peter O'Keefe and Tom Simington,
Irish stone bridges, history and heritage
(Dublin 1991).

O.W.S.

'Old' Society of Painters in Water-Colours,
annual exhibitions 1804-1881.

Ormond 1968

Richard Ormond,
'Daniel Maclise',
Burlington Magazine,
vol. 110, (1968), pp. 685-93.

Paris 1989

La Revolution Française et L'Europe 1789-1799,
Grand Palais, Paris, 1989.

Pyle 1970

Hilary Pyle,
Jack B. Yeats, a biography,
(London 1970).

Hilary Pyle,
Jack B. Yeats in the National Gallery of Ireland,
(Dublin 1986).

Pyle 1986

Seán Rothery,
The Shops of Ireland,
(Dublin 1978).

Rothery 1978

Royal Academy, London,
annual exhibitions from 1769.

R.A.

Royal Hibernian Academy, Dublin,
annual exhibitions from 1826.

R.H.A.

Royal Society of Painters in Water-Colours, London,
annual exhibitions from 1882.

R.W.S.

Jeanne Sheehy,
Walter Osborne,
(Ballycotton 1974).

Sheehy 1974

Jeanne Sheehy,
The Rediscovery of Ireland's Past: the Celtic Revival 1830-1930,
(London 1980).

Sheehy 1980

Frederic G. Stephens,
Memorials of William Mulready, R.A.,
(London 1890).

Stephens 1890

William Stokes,
The Life of George Petrie,
(London 1868).

Stokes 1868

Walter Strickland,
A Dictionary of Irish Artists,
2 vols., (Dublin and London 1913).

Strickland 1913

U. Thieme & F. Becker,
Allgemeines Lexicon der Bildenden Künstler,
vol. xvi, (Leipzig 1923).

Thieme-Becker 1923

John Turpin,
'The Irish background to Daniel Maclise',
The Capuchin Annual,
(1970), pp. 190-92.

Turpin 1970

Turpin 1986

John Turpin,
'The Dublin School of Landscape and Ornament 1800-1854',
Irish Arts Review, vol. 3, no. 2,
(Summer 1986), pp. 45-52.

W.S.I.

The Watercolour Society of Ireland,
annual exhibitions from 1870.

Webber 1972

Michael Webber,
'English Watercolours: the Leger Galleries',
Arts Review,
(2 December 1972).

Webster 1970

Mary Webster,
Francis Wheatley,
(London 1970).

White 1967

Christopher White,
'Master Drawings from Dublin',
Master Drawings,
vol. 4, (1967), pp. 411-12.

Wilson 1964

Arnold Wilson,
'Drawings by William Mulready, R.A. 1786-1863',
Connoisseur,
vol. 157, (November 1964), pp. 172-76.

Wynne 1972

Michael Wynne,
'Thomas Frye (1710-1762)',
Burlington Magazine,
vol. 114, (February 1972), pp. 78-85.

Wynne 1982

Michael Wynne,
'Thomas Frye (1710-1762) reviewed',
Burlington Magazine,
vol. 124, (October 1982), pp. 624-28.

Yeats 1912

Jack Yeats,
Life in the West of Ireland,
(London 1912).

Yeats 1944

John Butler Yeats, letters to his son William Butler Yeats and others,
edited by Joseph Hone, (New York 1944).